Made in the USA
Las Vegas, NV
21 February 2021

18312112R00176

me when I check into bliss. Touched by her husband, Sol Dolinger, a good man. Touched by my father who taught me the art of forgiveness and his wife, Suzanne Habib, who is forgiveness and love personified. Touched by my Grandma Sally for being a Bad Bitch Goddess, with assets. Touched by all my animals, here and there, who are healers, guides, and angels. And touched by Kenza Lee Schnur, the sprite who rocked my world. Kenza, my niece, my soul sister, a little Bad Bitch and fellow Good Witch. I miss you and reach for your love every day–until we meet again.

Bad Bitch

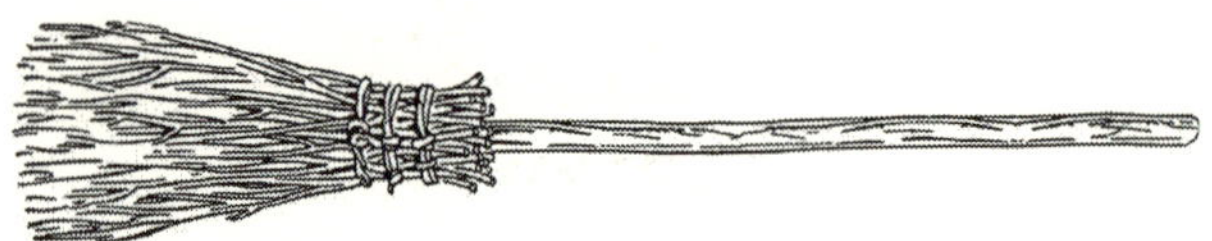

Good Witch

Malorie Barbaria

ISBN 9780979414336

For information: AbracadabraBook@gmail.com

For my niece,

Kenza Lee Schnur

(10.11.1993–07.08.2017)

My Light Being Sister,

a fellow Badass Bitch and a Dang Good Witch,

here and there.

Contents

Pre–Her-Story

"My inner devil loves to have fun; she makes me feel so good!"

I got away with being a Bad Bitch for years. Until I didn't. Being bad is titillating and packs a punch, but when its dark side goes out of control, it can be quite harmful, especially when it comes back around to knock your lights out. I could give you a million excuses why, but the most important one is this: When I was little, my mother told me, "You're only good when you're sleeping." You might think this a hideous thing to say to a child, but she'd say it with a slight smile on her face, as if she were proud. As the bad girl among three well-bred sisters, my mother had a mischievous *let's see what I can get away with* edge, and I inherited it. Having many personas, my mother displayed them like charms. Her bitch aspect amused me the most, for it was powerful and, once I tried it on, addicting.

The arrogant attitude that no one else matters but you, we all have it to a degree, but when we don't give a shit about anyone else, we're in trouble. It's shocking that this kind of vein could run through an enlightened human, distorting everything and taking them down. It happened to

me; I was taken down. Being a nasty bitch will do that. It will accelerate karma and eventually knock you off your high horse. At first, it seemed to be a curse, though it became a blessing after I was rescued by the Good Witch.

There's a Her-Story around my tale . . .

Once upon a time there was a young girl who grew up in a *Breakfast at Tiffany's* era, during a very charming time to be alive in Manhattan. She held mysterious special powers, in that she could make things happen in her favor, though she had issues and anger was one of them. She looked like an angel, but when bothered, especially by other children, she was nasty and could fend for herself quite well. The toddler that took her shovel in the sandbox got hit over the head with her pail. A small child, she was incredibly strong and could hold a boy twice her size in a bear hug while she instructed her little brother to pour a can of Coke over his head. When her little brother was made fun of for throwing up on the camp bus, she ran up and down the aisles yanking the perpetrators' hair with all her might. After a while, other children would not dare to cross her because she'd established herself as a hellion.

Adults and teachers in school left her alone, so she was a contently happy child who devoured books and spent much time dreaming. She grew up caring little what others thought and driven to have her way she was considered a total bitch. Instead of being loved and adored in the ways she thought

she should have been, she was disliked and even hated, as this is what bitches attract. The transition from Bad Bitch to Good Witch happened while she was successfully selling real estate, as she publicly smiled but was a tyrant behind the scenes and labeled intolerant for telling clients the truth about what was wrong with their houses. She told buyers that they should just pay the price and be glad they got in when they did. Telling office administrators they were stupid and needed to do better, of course they hated her. In all honesty, she was mostly right about these things, but her delivery was a torpedo of rage over the fact that others were not on her frequency and had to be told what to do. Granted, she was her agency's unchallenged top producer though she was downright terrifying.

Despite being christened a bitch, she never lied or stole another broker's customers, nor did she cheat buyers or sellers. Well, maybe once, as a payback to a vile broker who stole her first deal, and she didn't get him back personally, it just karmically happened that his customers would only work with her–and she let it. Mostly an honest realtor playing in a sandbox with a bunch of piranhas; she knew how to slay them. We might think bitches, liars, and self-serving people get away with it, but when their karma is up for clearing, they will come to terms. Rage, when it's fulfilled its purpose by screaming bloody murder at offenders, will always turn back towards its beholders to slap them in the face. Suddenly nothing works out; we find ourselves in a Hell-hole looking in the mirror and seeing harsh truths. It's our wake-up call to stop acting out and

start transforming what needs consideration and shifting.

Bad Bitch grew up with psychic abilities; a defined sixth sense with an endowment to read the future because it was always flashing in her direction. She could see through the veils and read all the buried stories that others had hidden. She could divine antidotes to people's rash wrong turns and often procured miracles where needed. As she grew older, in her teenage years, she read energy fields around people, intuiting what they needed, though she scared others by blurting out truths that cut to the bone. The harsh realities she portrayed moved energy to alleviate issues, yet still her edgy expression was a problem. Her special powers shape-shifted reality as she subliminally found diamonds in the rough and spotlighted them, which brought people's afflictions out and into resonance, so they could heal. Since she was not always nice about the delivery of these magical gems, they were perceived as attacks.

Prior to selling real estate, Bad Bitch had been a hair and makeup artist in Manhattan. She was a craftswoman at enhancement: rock stars, models, artists, and prolific beings all came to her salon. Touching her client's heads, haircut aside they would find themselves leaving her salon feeling highly transformed. She read their energy fields as she cut their hair, not knowing herself this was strange, as just by seeing their stories float by it seemed she was dissolving them. Certainly, none of this was clearly defined, that she was a healer as she waved her magic comb—it just happened.

Hired for photo shoots, she told editors they were not

original, photographers they were not daring enough and models that beauty was not everlasting. She told a famous actress that she'd lost touch with her sexuality and was holding herself back. They argued over the heavy black eyeliner Bad Bitch applied. The actress said it made her look like a hooker; Bad Bitch left the dressing room, refusing to remove it. That day's photographer, the very daring Robert Mapplethorpe, was waiting, so the actress had no choice but to go on set with the applied sultry black eyeliner. Mapplethorpe complimented her, and this very respectable actress suddenly fell into a provocative energy field where a wanton woman emerged. It was a side of herself she'd never explored, and with this newly sparked sensuality, she went on to win an Academy Award for one of the steamiest art films ever made.

At another shoot, an unknown teenage model read Bad Bitch poetry between takes, and Bad Bitch, with her special powers, asked the youngster to reveal her dream, which was to become an actress. They both imagined it happening, and within a year the model appeared in one of the most profound films made, alongside one of the greatest actors of the time. She then went on to become one of the most well-known actresses in her own right. Since Bad Bitch was a truth-slayer, some people were put off. The issue was that she—the girl with special powers—lacked a censor and left a trail of pushed buttons in her wake.

As karma would have it, even good people with special powers who have not been mindful will be taken to the underworld and spanked by their own nastiness. Bad Bitch

went face-to-face with herself; people turned on her and wished her ill. Things appeared not to work, she lost her mojo, and almost lost her life. A healer she worked with was worried that Bad Bitch would not survive what the healer had called her initiation. During this rite of passage, as she fell into her looking glass, a door of transformation had opened that shattered Bad Bitch's ego, humiliating her to humbleness. Her ground shook, and for a decade she was continually forced to face harsh truths about herself. That's how long it took for her to become self-conscious, to clearly reflect, and to live in service within her highest accord.

Others were not forgiving right off, and an important lesson she'd learned was never to take revenge or wish ill on her perpetrators, but to protect herself by continuing to raise her vibration. Since the laws of karma deliver exactly what we are doing back to us, it was arduous to send love and blessings to her foes when all she wanted was to send daggers. She understood that raising her vibration was all that was necessary, so it became her new practice. Her karmic ledger had brought her to a place that smacked her around, but as soon as she adopted kindness, she became so compassionate that many days she found herself in constant prayer.

Since she'd always identified with good witches, Bad Bitch adopted this benevolent essence to work through her latest transformation with. The days of nasty bitch diminished as being the Good Witch, she reclaimed her powers and vowed to use them in the highest ways. Once

again, her charms returned, and since Bad Bitch evolved into her enchanted self while still successfully selling real estate, her co-workers dubbed her *The Real Estate Witch.* They found pots of money hidden in the Feng Shui abundance corners of the office and there were always candles sticking out of her purse. She'd taped mantras and power statements to her computer, phone and wallet, and carried sage everywhere, as she constantly smudged houses and people, making real estate miracles happen. Suddenly feeling impelled to write her wisdom on mysticism, she authored ***The Abracadabra Series***, three books channeling evolved transcriptions that she herself had to follow. What she'd written centered on fearlessness, faith, transformation, forgiveness, love, and staying in the highest authenticity. The books became survival guides that cut through many veils, into a soul connection of direct guidance.

As fortune would have it, this woman with special powers had emerged as a good witch at a time when it's mandatory and urgent to resonate higher and be in service to a greater good. Bad Bitch had never previously acknowledged her inner Good Witch, for inherently she remembered being burned at the stake in other lifetimes, as her nastiness was being burned to ash in this one. This transformation into the Good Witch was like having the mother of her dreams guide her into her power. Her real mother was undermining and competitive, a handed-down trait, but Good Witch renounced this dynamic in herself. She looked into her crystal ball and saw the future she wanted to be part of and

revved up her broom to get there.

First, she had to open the wound to heal it, and this made her embrace all of her aspects—yes, including Bad Bitch. When the two finally merged, it was a perfect spark, a yin-yang dynamic: the concept of dualism; darkness and light, good and bad, chaos and peace. The duality was complementary, it interrelated as night needs day to continue on, thus our oppositions bring us into balance. It's an internal evolution to understand a shit storm as giving us the ability to come to peace within ourselves. We learn that by embracing our oppositions, we're juxtaposing all things into one force, to be used as potential. Dark times call for light, and we all have it within ourselves to become light bearers. So, when things seem horribly wrong, it's not a time to get lost slaying what's not good enough. Instead it's a time to uncover and bring about what is. Seeing it this way, we transpose into our best essence to hold our own, and the Good Witch is that essence for me.

ABOUT (BITCH) FACE

In the modern business world, women have been forced to use an edgy bitch modality when coming up against men; they're then deemed threatening while men acting similarly are admired as smart. The word *bitch* means female dog; aggressive women are commonly identified with dogs in heat. We're not at all like dogs in heat—we're actually females on fire who take no shit! The great bitches of this world stand out, not back, and they call out bullshit even on themselves when they've fallen into a nasty bitch mode. They're loyal like dogs sensing evil and will attack when necessary. You definitely want a bitch on your side.

My style of bitch is like Artemis, the Greek Goddess of the hunt. Artemis was a wildly magical, uncontrolled, forceful deity who traveled with a pack of wild dogs (and was even known to turn into one when necessary). She was the huntress who relieved women of disease, even taking on certain illnesses to alleviate them. So maybe I'm a button pusher, but my bitch mode is coming from a heart place, with an Artemis dynamic that cares. If I told you Bad Bitch brings on disruption leading to enlightenment, would you believe me? Bad Bitch has forcefully, energetically, smacked

others in the face, only to get them to hear helpful truths, and for that I am truly sorry.

All personas have a dark and light side; our light side is our hero's edge and our dark side is our shadow. My bitch's hellish shadow persona was set up to be slain when her out of control nastiness shipped her off to Karmageddon. It was her uncontrolled frustration that caused her retribution, which reflected her own nastiness back to her and took her down. As far as karma goes, most nasty bitches attract a kill-the-bitch dynamic, which is quite a drag when there are radical feminists out there banging a gong on truths. When a bitch goes down, others gloat how they got the bitch, but bitches usually rise again. I did. If it sounds like a fairy tale, it was one: there were demons, angels, wizards, shamans, and ghosts of the past, all hanging out with me. I did battle, went to Hell, danced with the Gods, and finally climbed out of that hole to begin again, my temperament being more saintly than bitchy.

I can't blame my bad bitchiness on my mother, nor can I say that being in the real estate world (a.k.a shark tank) awakened her, as I've always had her in me. After all, she's an asset when I need to take a stand, because she thinks outside the box and challenges the concept of *No*. She's also a survivor who's been through tough times and knows how to maneuver her way into a miracle zone. She's my ally and I would *never* abandon her, especially when I need her advice. Once we are co-conspirators with ourselves, we join sides with our creative force, as intuitiveness is our power place.

By the way, it was my bad bitch that decided to write this book and expose herself. She took herself to the top of the Fu*k-it plateau and leaped. Not leaving any aspect of herself behind, she embraced all of herself—and it was this embrace that she flew on.

Being a nasty bitch is a story we believe, just as some actors think they really *are* the role they're playing. When the movie is over, they have to snap out of it. In the same way, I snapped out of the bitch story because I needed a new one. It's our nature to try on personas like children in nursery school where we get to be the doctor, nurse, daddy, bunny, flower, or whatever we imagine. Beyond playing with personalities and identities, we find out who we are and what works. My nasty bitch was a force field I aggressively used to get my way. Still, she's outspoken and does not question herself over every little thing—and since her merger with Good Witch, the duo can afford to take chances, because their clean-up crew is exemplary.

Appropriately, Bad Bitch learns from her failures, which she deems as necessary teachings, so she is not taken aback to learn the hard way. The shadow is what's up right now, and on a grand scale it's slapping us all in the face, while on a personal level it's saying: ***Deal With Me Now***, or we're not going anywhere good. So here we are, gyrating while embracing our wounds, our anger, our pain and our traumas, to transform ourselves through all of it. It's a gift when the curtain comes down and we have to confront ourselves, even if we must crawl on our knees to an appointment with our divinity. The story is

that from one day to the next, my bitch party was on the line. I wondered why my framework was working against me, while everything I'd built my castle on collapsed. The only place left for me to anchor myself into was my metaphysical mainstay. It felt like I went to Hell, though I was really on a date with the shadow side of my light being and once we began to dance together, I came back.

I've always found it misguided when powerful women are considered bitches in a bad way; like the ones passing judgement don't have a dark side. It's reminiscent of the old days, when women with powers were presumed witches and burnt at the stake. I must remind you that many of them were healers and women of God. These days, women who have the balls to play around with identities while they challenge stupidity and the status quo are considered bitches, when they're actually forceful women calling out weakness, lies, and wrongdoings. We, the bitches of this world, Stand Out! Some of us are unconscious, others are furious, I was just nasty. It depends on what we are using this persona for, as it's a fine line between dysfunction and enlightenment. My inner bitch has a sixth sense; she sees through the veils and is quite wise. She loves opposites and often reminds me that the antonym of *Bitch* (according to the Thesaurus) is *Saint*. I've dubbed my inner bitch, Saint Bitch, for as destiny would have it, she was nearly slain and could only survive by coming into her Saintly Self.

Mind you, even though my mother told me I was only good when I was sleeping, I *knew* I was dang good and

figured I was waking up to take my good self with me. We're all in this process of waking up as we traipse in and out of many levels of consciousness, while reasoning with our opinions and inner personas that have different agendas. My bitch created the ally she needed in herself, the one with the remedies to get through these insane times. Since she's morphed her nasty side into the selfhood of the Good Witch, she's merged her shadow into a light field, so now we're bitchin' good witchin'. By the way, in the Urban Dictionary, *bitchin'* is described as not just great, but badass fine.

PART ONE

THE PREMISE OF GOOD WITCHERY

"Click your heels, make your statement, own it as if your life depended on it, and live it forward in your mind first."

When I was a teenager, I went to a witchcraft shop on the upper west side of Manhattan to buy red candles in the shape of a man and a woman. With those candles, I worked a spell on a couple I knew, to break them up. I carved their names into the figures, lit the candles, and moved them farther apart daily. After three days, the spell worked, and they separated. I did this because I wanted to be with the fellow—only to realize a day later that I really didn't want him at all. This was black magic and I never got over the fact that I'd practiced it and was shamefully sorry. Granted, the fellow was a jerk and I probably did the girl a big favor, but I was messing with other people's lives for selfish reasons.

In the phase when I was playing with power and learning how forceful intention can be, I understood that making things happen is possible, but selfishness and bad intentions have their own laws of cause and effect. These laws state that karma will always come back around to be dealt with. Back then, I hated that I'd cast that spell and learned not to mess

with things for selfish reasons—a vow I promptly forgot and had to relearn many times over. When we're only interested in fulfilling our desires, we're quite busy playing marbles with our destiny, though the question is: What is our real destiny and do we let it unfold or do we override inevitability and force our circumstances? The answer is: It has to become a dance where we do both.

I'm one of those have-to-have-it-now types, so anything in my way is fodder to be bulldozed. For me, the word *No* means *try another way*, so I won't give up until I've exhausted all possibilities. Living in a *my-way* reality is dynamically good for making things happen but being aligned with a universal energy field is far more magical. It was not until I got slammed over and over and finally brought to my knees that I realized I was in a partnership with a power way higher than my own earthly self. I call this higher power the Divine Spirit. Divine Spirit has rules based on integrity, so being merely self-serving doesn't work. What works is being in tune with the highest good one can muster.

As a Realtor Witch who is always thinking ten steps ahead, I would replay the outcomes of my maneuvers to decide which ones promised result. Competition was involved, and I had to get the deal. I would push hard on the buyers who were usually in agreement with me, as they wanted to win too. One couple had looked at over a hundred homes for sale with various brokers, me included. Though when I'd shown them the house of their dreams, they didn't listen to me and bid too low. The owner took an immediate dislike to them and refused to sell

them his house, period.

The buyer's wife was literally crying on Main Street in Bridgehampton about how she'd finally found her dream home and could never have it. I told her to hang in and that I would not give up on getting her this house. I then came up with another house that I knew the stubborn seller would love more than his house. When I called to tell him about it, he said, "No, I'm not interested in buying another house right now." He then hung up. I called him back, told him the address, and suggested he just drive by it. Calling me later that day, he wanted to see this other house and upon doing so, immediately fell for it. I then told him to forget about how he felt about his buyers and just sell them the house at his price. He did, and we closed on both houses on the same day one month later.

If I had sat around and waited for the universe to fix the deal, it would never happen. So yes, I was a manipulator, but the universe was in an agreeable mood that day. Being manipulative in any sense is about getting lost in believing things have to go a certain way. In this case, the highest magic was present in maneuvering all the parties into their new residences, while I was maneuvering money into my bank account. I always played to win, and the winning edge was where things got tricky, because I was ruthless. It was my gut that was intentionally ruthless and when I sensed another broker was not honorable, I went around them to expose them.

I once sensed an exclusive broker was not presenting my

offer because she was presenting her own buyer's lower offer. So, I put my buyer's full price offer in writing and had my assistant drive it to the seller's house and present it directly to him. He immediately took it and we won the deal. I was right that the other broker was cheating her seller and me. That's the problem with cheating a psychic realtor: I knew. That other broker could have lost her license, but we let her bad behavior go because to me, being caught was enough.

It probably would have been better if I had used niceness as a manipulation in my real estate business, maybe I would not have attracted the wave of resentment that came at me and eventually knocked me off my high horse. The truth is I wanted to get off that horse anyway; I was tired and ready to get magical with my life. That's when things began to not work out, the market changed, and a wave of difficult buyers and sellers showed up. At times shit doesn't work out because it's not meant to, but my Bad Bitch doesn't get it, won't allow it, and pushes, while the Good Witch stands back to see what's unfolding before messing with stuff. She knows there's a power place in all things, and if you stop moving the dirt around, it will appear.

The stakes got higher and after over a decade of winning I no longer had it in me to play the game. My new plan was to show up for the way the Universe had arranged things and tap into the highest elevation with them. Divine Spirit will always hold our best interests at heart, so while we're in the midst of struggling, this intense need to manipulate comes from our lack of trust. Eventually after all our shenanigans, we get put on the line to have faith in our higher power, the

team player who knows better. By investing in what our imagination (holy mind) brings forth, we are in alliance with a new plan. And even if our course of action is still unknown and only a feeling of something that has not yet arrived, we get buzzed by the anticipation of grace. What's buzzing is the new, enlightened energy field locking into our DNA, as we're upgrading to a higher dimension known as the fifth.

While things are formulating in the mystery of life it can be uncomfortable when we're being forced to go with a new flow. When I feel a wave of an undermining edge coming at me, it means it's time to stop everything and assess who I am now. Oftentimes we fall into the who-did-what hole, and who sucks for being a creep, when in reality others do what they do and what matters is how we handle it. We've all spent time defining our enemies, when it was actually aspects of our own selves taking us down. There were times I even considered discomfort an enemy, until I realized it was a shape-shifting necessity and the sooner I relaxed around it, the faster it would move. Crazy to understand discomfort as an ally!

Bad Bitch would write my enemies' names on paper, put the papers in Tupperware containers with water and freeze them. At one point, my freezer was full of Tupperware containers. I was freezing bad energy yet still there was always more bad energy arriving as I had not yet frozen my own. I was further messing with the nature of cause and effect by maneuvering magic. What happened was, I worried about stopping all the negativity coming at me, when the only real

protection is to get oneself onto a higher vibration. The Good Witch was hanging around, whispering innuendos, showing me other options. One of her best strategies is to surrender and wait out the shit storms, while not getting covered in them.

One morning, back in my hair and makeup artist life, I was on my way to a photo shoot, and while I was late and hailing a taxi, a flock of pigeons dumped bird shit all over me. I humbly arrived at my job covered in it. A kind stylist helped to wash it off and gave me a designer outfit to wear and keep. My first thought after getting barraged in that slime was go home and hide, while my next thought was: Shit happens, keep going! Granted, when shit happens, I wonder what I did to deserve it. My inner Bad Bitch runs to the mirror to see if she's still the fairest of all, only to see Good Witch staring back, saying: "Shit is a sign of release, release your emotional crap." This does not mean surrender to accepting what feels like crap, it means surrender to changing ourselves through it. I then heard my mother saying, "*Birds shitting on you is good luck,*" and decided to go with that.

Can it be good luck to be shit upon? It can, if we use the experience for all it's worth to grow out of it. Seeing an opening for escalated consciousness takes us out of victim mode, which is the poor-me zone we react from. *Me, mine, all about me, what about me?* We can be stuck in a cage of ME-isms, while the *I Am* consciousness waits, knocking for us to open the door. Liberation isn't on the other side of the door,

it's in us opening the door. The *I Am* consciousness brings us right to the nothing and the everything all at once. Try on the *I Am*, sit with it, see where it takes you–you'll find it's a bliss zone.

Bitches are great at building walls. They live in their own special VIP club and think they can delineate their world, but this only works until it doesn't. We can't thrive for the long haul in a nothing-but-me-matters reality, as actuality will eventually break through to show us how things really are. Once the walls come down, we feel everything we've ever held at bay until we get to our grief. Our grief is the transformer that tears us open in order for us to become *wabi-sabi* masters, the ones who seal the cracks in our broken hearts with gold. So during the times when things go terribly wrong, when we're doing battle, slaying demons, and hopelessness slips in sideways to drag us to its bad party, remember we did not come here to be lost in negative illusions–and that's why our falsities are cracking apart.

Sorrow comes with a directive on how to heal through it. The objective is to stand right where we are to see the pertinent message that has been left in the trail of our pain. I had to stop screaming about how badly I was hurt, to find hurt's healing indications. Cracked open and psychically in pieces, I was being shown what was venerable in my hardship. The five stages of grief being: denial, anger, bargaining, depression and acceptance, each layer is doing surgery to clear us. Once we get to acceptance, we begin to see clearly enough to find our way to a healing.

Wabi-sabi denotes the perfections in the imperfection of life, considering impermanence as a natural evolution. The Japanese art form, *Kintsugi*, displays the cracks in broken ceramics by mending them with gold. The golden veins that hold those cracks together signal that we must esteem the highlighted fault-lines instead of devaluing them. The embodiment of *wabi-sabi* is about embracing what's broken and unpredictable—to define the beauty in it. Consider that the *wabi-sabi* of love is about how we celebrate love's journey, even when it takes us everywhere we never wanted to go but completes us. And thus, we pause to focus on the blessings in how things are as opposed to how things should be. It's not easy.

Evolving through the mastery of intense lessons gives us the ability and courage to hold our own no matter what. A shift is happening behind the scenes, which empowers us to move from victim to victor. It's hard, we're exhausted, some of us are grieving the past. This lifetime is like a fire walk, where we're walking into our holy land as all else burns up. At times it feels like hell, though it's not distorted to still have a belief that we're in the right place because what's sacred is still holding us through all of it.

My brother asked me a really important question that took me weeks to answer. He was in searing grief over the death of his twenty-three-year-old daughter from a drug overdose. He asked me why did he have to live through the painful loss of the two most influential women in his life to drug addiction? The other woman was our mother, which

made it hard to decipher the answer as I was too close to the situation, but when you pull way back there's always another perspective. My brother had spent years successfully amassing his fortune, which now felt meaningless to him. Even though it came through this hardship of such loss, he felt closer to God than ever before. He meditated daily, joined a grief group, and saw his beautiful daughter around him in signs.

I asked my brother to imagine the possibility of both women, his daughter and our mother taking a birth in this lifetime to bring him closer to the hero within himself. I said, "Imagine them doing what they did so you could come to be aligned with your divine spirit and live the rest of your life in your highest truth, all bullshit aside." My brother is still thinking about this, as coming to peace around these painful experiences isn't done alone. We must come into a spiritual consciousness to heal our searing pain, and it's a process of how deep into trauma we can go to remove it. Our journey will go where it needs to give us what we need, and often we find ourselves broken, lost in a nether world. The way out is for us to face the undeniable truth and reinvent ourselves from it.

Bad Bitch is brilliant at maneuvers and operations; she can assess a situation and figure it out quickly. Looking for meaning is my natural agenda, as behind the scenes our higher essence is banging on our doors and ringing our bells to be acknowledged. Meanwhile higher essence is clearing negative energy that have dark implants; it's healing our broken hearts and divining goodness. The Good Witch is in

tune and hears things that can't be heard by human ears, like the singing of lost souls we need to guide us home. We all receive messages in subtle ways, such as a broken branch showing us that life's too heavy and we're carrying too much. Or maybe a car battery becomes a messenger when it dies by telling us to stay home for now. Maybe the cats are fighting, attacking each other, which reminds us to calm the f*ck down. The orbs that float by are telling us we're graced by sacred deities that prance around us as helpers, while the clouds draw pictures that speak to us. We're not lost in la-la land, we're awake in ah-ha land.

In the times when things are not working out, I wonder if I'm being cursed. There are some dark witches in my town, practitioners of black magic who don't wish me well. Of course, I have frozen their spells to the point where they are just silly women with bad intentions going nowhere. The morning I woke up to a bedroom full of yellow jackets flying around, I wondered if this was a new unholy blight (like a curse that penetrated my protection barrier), or just a displaced hive in the wall? The pest control man came to remove the hive.

I looked up Bee Spirit Medicine, which describes pollinating new ideas and miracles. In reading about bee's wings, aerodynamically a bee should not be able to fly, but they do. It's because they've gone beyond limitations and they work in communities to manifest abundance. I am a loner of sorts, who steps in and out of society because I'm always drawn back into solitary. I need space to dream and I wondered if the bees in my

bedroom sent a message for me to step into a more community sourced lifestyle. I thereupon realized my real community is not necessarily in human form in that it exists in relation with my spiritual allies. These invisible friends told me to stay connected with them and they would show me a new flight pattern, navigating me to my nectar. The flying insects in my bedroom were a blessing, which reminded me to keep my buzz going.

Our dreams are novellas of the past, present, and future all talking to us at once. They direct us to the avenues where our spirit guides have left boons for us. We are led to herbs and medicines, to other loving beings, to books and healers. And once we commune with our angels, ancestors, and with nature and higher spirit, we come to understand that we're all connected. In our most difficult times, feeling lost is a time to delve deep into the exact predicament for messages. I've lost my mojo, I can't do things the way I've done in the past, but I don't yet know the new way. I'm in limbo as the exit door is flashing and I'm reluctant to open it. I open it a crack and peek into a divined future and suddenly I'm in a place where new ideas are on the table. I've dropped into an undertaking of something coming to be and feel bursts of gratitude for everything—even the hard stuff.

I once had a soul sister who was my true best friend, she was there at my wedding, and at the birth of my son. When she was lost professionally, I escorted her into a career that skyrocketed. I was there when her son passed away from an overdose. We had been through a lot together and I loved her. Then one day she just stopped talking to me, as if I'd

done something terrible to her, which I never did. To say it hurt was an understatement: it burned. As the years went by, I would think, *Good riddance. I really don't need a friend like that.* In real truth, I missed her. Once in our twenties, we'd made a promise to each other, that when we were old ladies, we would sit on a park bench laughing together. One night I had a dream that this friend came to visit me as if nothing ever happened—and we were sitting on that bench laughing. I woke up sad, but then I realized I still wished her well, even if it was just in spirit and so I became grateful for the good times of our friendship. Our bond might have died in reality, but not in my heart—and admitting this was enlightening. Good Witchery doesn't dwell on what's "bad," but instead focuses on what's cherished, as this kind of thinking liberates us from bad.

A natural response to our essential virtuous nature is to embrace an enlightened state. At times, our virtuousness is ignored, we've all done things we're not proud of. To ask for forgiveness (even just from ourselves) for our past trespasses, healing energy moves towards us. And once we move into conduct with ethical principles, supreme rectitude becomes dominant. Here, we're addressing our deep-seated character that goes beyond triggers to significant issues that demand importance. Our ethical principles are not ruled, nor determined by organizations or cultures, instead they're self-defined by what's sublimely correct for us personally. We decide what they are!

We're now living in times that demand an active wake up

call, a snap-out-of-it resonance where the possibility of being enlightened is real. While timing is everything, a student once asked a Guru: "How long will it take to become enlightened—months, years, a lifetime, many lifetimes?" The Guru responded, "You are already enlightened, you just forgot—all you need to do is wake up." Accordingly, in a blink we can conceivably be enlightened. How crazy that it's just a matter of being so? Once again, we decide!

The premise of Good Witchery acknowledges our power and revolves around using it in the highest ways. We delve down deep inside our psyche—past our ego, past our inner child, through our shadow, to find the highest order where our power place is. Bad Bitch became needy during a dark time and was looking for assurances. Our soul connection circumvents neediness and wakes us up to be one in relation with the true essence of self. We get hit with a wake-up moment when it's time to go boundless—pushed past old beliefs into our ancient wisdom sanctuary. This inner knowledge tells us to own our power, unlearn all rhetoric, de-droid from opinions, and check into our passion.

Henceforth, when we hone into our intuition and our soul's influence, we can blow alchemy into any reality. And once we're in partnership with the Cosmic Divine Spirit of the Universe, we offer our best shot and then let the magnetism of the cosmos decide how it goes. Being liberated from the worry of constantly figuring it all out, we're relieved of trying every which way to make things happen. So, as we drop the desires, our resistance and maneuvers to connect in

with our highest, magical, badass self, we shift. There is supreme liberation as we no longer need to fit in—we're already in and that's how we come out—to ourselves.

I was recently interviewed by a co-op board, as they needed to decide if I could move into a building I loved. At first, I came up with an act around being exactly the type of person I thought they were looking for. Then I decided to be myself and trust that if I didn't fit in, I wasn't meant to be there. It was a long interview with non-stop questions that I honestly answered. I then questioned them about things that seemed too ruled for me. After calming me down about some of their restrictions, they welcomed me to their building. Similarly, welcoming the authenticity in ourselves is our first step in trusting that we're good as we are—even with our imperfections. By embracing ourselves, self-love becomes the metaphysical broom we fly on.

Commitment to the highest and holiest integrity in ourselves is our Good Witch premise saying: "*I will stand in power with myself, believing in my magic and the alchemy that surrounds all that I am and all that I need.*" If you repeat this statement three times, you will start to feel it resonate energetically. We are tapping into a charged calibration where creation manifests. In manifestation mode, we wander around with great respect as our own personal shoppers—although we don't grab at things. Instead, we get into a divine state and wait for things to call out to us as an offering. Once we have collected our goods, we return home to implement them into our life. We are privileged to come

from a place of enlightened enchantments, even while stepping on cracks and passing through waves of darkness. Since once we've owned our power, we're no longer under any influence, which leaves us to function at full capacity in Good Witch glory.

BEING ENLIGHTENED
Waking Up in A Crazy World

"A blink into a higher reality defines the moment and removes the confusion–so the lessons, the rituals, and the symbols, all become forms of enlightenment."

A heightened state of knowingness that goes beyond the poppy field we've gotten lost in is our original state of being, before we were imposed upon. Being enlightened is our natural birthright and it's high time to reclaim it. My niece, as a child, would always tell my brother that he was not acting even one percent Gandhi when he was angry with her. My brother loved the essence of Gandhi. At five years old, his daughter subliminally understood the nature of the goodness that Gandhi embodied–and that her dad was not being it. Her statement would always stop my brother in his tracks, even if it were just to laugh at himself. We all have personas that we play with and then we have our enlightened selves hanging around waiting for us to join them at their most mystical and scintillating party. Whether we receive an invitation depends upon how lost in certain identities we've

gotten and how ready we are to give them up.

As a yogi, I had a teacher who definitely had sparks of enlightenment but was not considerate and seemed to be a social climber. I noticed this when my teacher's friend came and taught a yoga class and after, I had an enlightening chat with the substitute teacher, who then asked my teacher who I was. "*No One!*" replied my yoga teacher. Wow, this was revealing. I confronted my teacher and asked him why he said that. He tried to cover it up by saying it was a compliment but what he was really saying was that I was not important on the social ladder he was climbing, so therefore his friend shouldn't bother with me.

The pedestal I'd put him on came down in a crash, and finally it became a total gift to just simply go to yoga, do the practice, and be there in honor of my own spirit. This seeing behind the veil of my yoga teacher cleared my disciple persona, the part of me that wants to put other spiritually inclined people on an upper platform, instead of sitting in my own Bodhi wisdom temple with myself. The more we focus on the "who's who," while thinking enlightenment can be handed down by osmosis, the more time we're not participating in our own liberation. On the other hand, when encouraged by another's quality of life, we become inspired in the same way that one candle flame lights another.

Similarly, like a moth drawn to the light, once we begin to wake up to the fact that we're not this or that, we're in the frequency zone of enlightenment where being *No One* could

actually be a great compliment to an awakened being, but in an enlightened state, compliments don't matter. Even the Good Witch is a persona that my inner child likes to play with. And once we engage our authenticity, we discover our cosmic purpose so the persona we're playing with becomes a stepping-stone towards living our authentic life. I put the Good Witch hat on to shed some spiritual light on myself and to cultivate a way back into my highest resonance. It's certainly bringing me more good tidings than my nasty bitchiness. Meanwhile, Bad Bitch reminds me that if it weren't for her, there would be no dichotomy for me to come into enlightenment through. Still, she's grateful I calmed her nastiness down, so her beautiful badass self could shine through.

The Tao Te Ching says: *Knowing others is intelligence; knowing yourself is true wisdom. Mastering others is strength; mastering yourself is true power.* This calls for self-examination, which makes no excuses and doesn't pussyfoot around as it explores our motives, because it's on an expedition to decipher the truth for us when we can't find it. We might wrestle with excuses and explanations but none of that matters when it's time to get real. The deeper into ourselves we go, the closer we come to the nothing, which is a scary place at first, for as the Tao says: *The path into the light seems dark.* It's dark because we are in the process of freeing ourselves from the status quo; the need for approval, our insecurity, lack of faith, anxiety, striving, trying to be good, and our conditioning.

Bad Bitch went to a dark place and sat around ranting about what was not fair. Once I decided it wasn't an issue of what's fair or not, but rather an exploration of an energy dynamic that Bad Bitch was holding, I saw the darkness I was stuck in. Just seeing the truth of things, beyond the actual things, elevated me out of there. So, when actuality is not being kind, when things are going crazy, when life is a never-ending rocky road and when we scrutinize where inside ourselves, we hold onto these ways—then BOOM—we shift. This doesn't mean the car won't break down, there won't be arguments, annoyance, loss and heartbreak. It means we come at it from a higher place and it doesn't take us down.

Coming to these realizations, I fell into a state of liberated consciousness. The shift in consciousness was a new thought that separated me from who I thought I was. Suddenly I was no one but myself in connection with the cosmic universe and a light came on. All at once I was flooded with an array of enlightened perceptions—like if my vibration is magnetic and I hold it in an enlightened way, then things become enlightening instead of hellish. Imagine that! I do every morning, when I wake up and thank the Universe for another day to be part of this infinite abundance. Granted, in truth, I don't always wake up feeling this way; I might wake up with a full-blown anxiety attack over a nightmare. Still, I implant this *Thank You* statement into my psyche first thing, and it saturates and bleeds into my mind dreck to color the moment. Mastery is having the wisdom to override

what needs to be dropped with the ability to implant what's uplifting.

At lunch, an acquaintance expounded on her new healing technique that gave her the ability to heal an entire town in one session. I told her of the stress I was feeling that day and asked if she could remove it. We went off to the side of the restaurant, where she did her juju and in minutes my stress evaporated. Moments later, a magazine editor stopped by the table to say hello and I mentioned that they might feature this woman's new healing practice. The editor was game, when suddenly my healer friend went off on a tangent about how another healer featured in their magazine wasn't a real healer. I watched the entire energy field drop as the editor walked away and mentioned to my healer friend that it wasn't necessary to put another person down. She started making excuses and refused to own her mistake. My Bad Bitch felt like slapping her with some profound wake-up words, but the Good Witch knew that mentioning the need for self-examination was enough and left it at that. It's disappointing when people don't get how off-the-mark they are. At the same time, it's edifying to recognize that we no longer act in those same unenlightened ways.

Many times, a moment of enlightenment requests that we do the exact opposite of what we were inclined to do. The wicked witch is threatened and believes she needs those ruby slippers. The Good Witch is busy clicking her heels together, while the wicked witch is busy striving to score due to her insecurity. There comes a point where we have to stop trying

to kill the wicked witch and just hand over the slippers. Ms. Wicked is really the lost version of us, and to be in harmony with her, we must be givers. Ms. Wicked won't be able to maneuver in those slippers anyway, not until she raises her vibration. She can click her heels together until the cows come home, but still no go on the magic slippers working. We have to get into the zone that activates our magic and do a mental flip into our enlightenment.

Our Yellow Brick Road is really the path of finding out that even when we have no courage and we've acted brainless and heartless, by embracing these lost parts of ourselves, we restore our powers. How it happens is that there's no longer an inner enemy or a wrong way of being. Everything going on, including our own missteps, all become part of our tutelage when we're awake and using it as such. We come to know that we're not crazy for naught and it's all grist for the mill. For once we bridge our weaknesses into our strengths, we come to the realization that we've always had the ability to access our enlightenment—we just have to clear a way to reach it.

A client called to tell me that for no reason, a wondrous feeling overwhelmed her, it was as if the world was filled with magic. This is a woman who generally analyzes situations to the bone. We were working on selling her property together and normally she is quite involved in the process, but this time she surrendered it. She was open and that's when she felt the scintillating wave of energy flowing. Incidental things no longer mattered: what was happening in the market, the

criticisms from other brokers over the price. None of it had any power, and even though it was a down market at the time, her property had interest. A few days later, she was back to art directing how it should go and the good energy field around her sale collapsed. I appreciated watching this duality show, knowing it was a message that our teamwork no longer existed. I wanted to judge her for being an idiot, though instead I saw her as a messenger showing me how teamwork begins within. I then told her she needed to find another broker she could boss around, while her property has continued to sit on the market.

Being an ex-control freak, I know all about maneuvers and have learned that they do work, though only in a way that keeps us controlled in stuck-ness. Control freaks believe their way is the only way and that if they lock into it, it will protect them and keep them safe. It does keep them safely sealed in their own zipped lockdown. As a yogi, I know that going far is not about stretching into painful body mishaps; it's about the concept of stretching gently. We go a little farther and pause, we feel how it feels and then we go again. Then there are times we're grabbed and quickly flung into a higher comprehension. Subsequently there's always the catch-up where we must assimilate what happened.

Open-mindedness calls for detachment, which defines the difference between judging and exploring. Judging slams a door while exploring opens it. So, while traveling through dark tunnels it's best to stop reaching conclusions and scrutinize for what the darkness needs to enlighten itself.

Looking into our shadow with mindful intention gives us the liberal vision to clearly define what's needed for the darkness to come back into the light. While enlightenment is our live-in guru that's on call at all hours, the secret is that we must call its hotline to tap in, and then Abracadabra it delivers concepts and boons that expand our horizons.

Nasty bitch can't relax and is always on guard with her bag of tricks ready for what's coming. Her perspectives are befuddled because she lives in a wound zone where anxiety is her guru as she falls into the cracks of her hysterical mind. The fall off her high horse has knocked her lights out, so nothing makes sense. She can't make any decisions until she lets go of all ideas and lets herself just be, which makes her gyrate. Forced to finally surrender; she stops blaming and analyzing, staying in the moment. Bingo, suddenly a sublime flash of enlightenment captured her. Good Witch then stepped in and said, "We're now going this way." Granted, there are still wrestling matches that go on between them, but they're really exercises around what we go through to take ourselves higher.

Reading about a successful art dealer in Manhattan who was going off to jail for tax evasion, I remembered when I was a shampoo girl and washed her hair on numerous occasions. She wasn't famous then, but was on her way, and like a bitch she already owned her title. She once told me to scrub harder on her big head bursting with self-induced fabulousness. I was amused and never took her demanding demeanor seriously as from one bitch to another, it was something to be respected.

Reading about how she was publicly taken down in a modern-day witch hunt, I felt compassion for her.

Other bitches cheer when a fellow bitch goes down, because they're distorted and don't think of themselves as bitches. Usually, women with power are enlightened in many ways; this one, like me, turned into a wrong lane. I never stole and was just nasty in the playground, while she was both a thief and a nasty bitch. When a bitch gets taken down, it's usually because the universe has better plans for her. I visualized this woman coming into her enlightenment in prison, seeing her emerge as a healer and a representative of courage in facing oneself. Maybe I made this up (I did) but I'm empowering it for another sister I don't even know.

Our personal triumphs carry us across the trenches, so consider it an opportunity to act high-level whenever we're flung a can of worms. A desperate broker who was not getting a real estate deal done at the price his buyers wanted, lost his composure. He had a tantrum, started cursing and called me a psycho, so I just hung up. I thought about doing a whammy, turning him into a frog, along with many other nasty retaliations—it certainly was a struggle. I remembered that reactionary maneuvers trigger karma so instead, I threw love bombs at him. It was not easy but necessary to clear my own frame of mind. The next morning, he apologized and owned his behavior. I accepted his apology, but more than that, I was proud that I took myself higher. My victory over his negativity was probably what gave him the space to come and meet me there.

At the end of our lives, we look back on our stories and hopefully we love them, even with all our insane endeavors. I have great respect for all the hard times I've survived. I also have supreme consideration for how I've discerned the lessons that slapped me so hard that I lost my standing and crawled to a humble seat. All the downturns are limitation bulldozers that plug us into our higher consciousness. So, if this is not what's happening and you're on the floor crying about how bad things are, get up right now, brush yourself off and request enlightenment. It's about the extent to which we've broken down our limitations and how enlightened we become through them. Our stories constantly change as sparks of insight hide in every hardship, catastrophe, and transformation. These are gifts that bring us back to our original enlightened self. When we see it this way—we are seeing through the eyes of our enlightenment.

The Road to Enlightenment

- There's a spark of enlightenment inside you—fan it.
- Enlightening moments come from being expansive and not limiting our perceptions.
- When bad things happen, step into your enlightenment and deal with it from there.
- Imagine what it's like to live in an enlightened state and pretend to live there by asking yourself how enlightened beings act—then imitate them until you acquire the keys.

- Keep going through the sludge until you get to love—behind it is enlightenment.
- Resistance is a signal that we need to go deeper.
- Questioning our motives is the inquisition that leads to our enlightenment.
- Catching ourselves being egotistical is a turnaround to insight a.k.a enlightenment.
- When the ego causes us pain, consider that it's pushing us through the pain into our enlightenment, because the ego wants to wake up and transform itself as much as we do.
- Every time you come across a big load of ego on the road, even if you've stepped in it or have gotten yourself covered in it, bless yourself for the wake-up call and keep going.
- Going beyond presumption brings us to the blink of awareness.
- Enlightenment does not just happen in a blink—it <u>is</u> the blink.
- The struggle to reach a triumph is the worthiest encounter.
- To be in the magic is to recognize where it hides in all that exists.
- Once you've touched enlightenment you know it—and once you know it, you imbibe it.
- One second of enlightenment is an encyclopedia of wisdom.

- Even thinking about enlightenment puts us in its luminous zone.
- An enlightened knowing abounds in good vibrations, though where it leads might not be the most convenient prospect; still, it will be the most nurturing in the end.
- Drop all that you think you know and delve into the mystery of what you don't know; that's where our bodhi tree is.
- This journey through our shadow back to the light has many twists and turns, so when it gets dark and painful, relax knowing that everything turns a corner.
- Look for the answer in the question; if the question is enlightening, the answer is in there.
- Since we've arrived here enlightened and are now returning to enlightenment, consider everything in the middle as a stepping-stone from here to there.
- We all have access to a bodhi mind—by recognizing this we can awaken through anything.
- Don't waste time disagreeing, enlightenment cajoles transgressions beyond limitations.
- Our self-realization won't be handed down, only discovered.
- Consider the source behind the thinking mind and speak to it—this source is the higher self that is always on call.
- A heartfelt feeling is enlightenment speaking beyond all realities—open your heart.

- Delusion is ego hiding from its own enlightenment. Delusion causes pain, depression, anxiety, and fear, shutting us down. When we see it as a wake-up call, we awaken.
- Open your mind a crack; that crack is cosmic consciousness, so always look for the crack.
- Think of everything going on as connected to something else and know enlightenment is always in the something else.
- Enlightenment can't be defined, created, or sought; it can only be realized.
- The more bounteous moments of enlightenment that we bank on, the more in-balance we are with our supreme existence.
- Recognizing that we already have what we're looking for is the first spark.
- To see the divine in all things is the kindling of realization.
- Divinity has no favorites; it only bends towards those who favor it.
- So, even when things get rough, use whatever's going on to birth your holiness.
- This life is a dream, and to awaken in the dream is enlightenment.
- Honoring enlightenment is also enlightenment.

ENERGETIC IMPLANTS
Clearing Unfavorable Energy

"We are responsible for what we own!"

In the ways that a new tooth can be implanted into someone's jaw and be incorporated into our physical being, energetic implants are emotional slipstreams, being infused into our quantum field to be made manifest into real-world tangible phenomena. Case in point being that we don't suddenly see ourselves as "not good enough," this is a deeded entity, an inaccurate story that somewhere along the line someone–maybe a teacher, mother, father, or friend, had created by believing it. On a subliminal level their belief reflected this allegory back to us and on a subconscious plane we bought into that story. We bought it because it was implanted into our psychological psyche and auric field, so consider that the power of thoughts is like a wand, and every bad wish we send toward someone is flying at him or her like a dagger.

We all at times have tears in our auric field from our inner struggles, poor health, and emotional upheavals, and

this is when we're open for implants to easily be imposed upon us. Others not wishing us well, feelings of jealousy or competitiveness, holding anger and seeking revenge, all send targeted implants. We could tag this fiction as coming from an old wound, or a bad parent (a.k.a karmic predicament), but we don't suddenly show up at a job interview with a secret feeling that we're not good enough. What happened was an exterior thought form got into us like a virus; it implanted this feeling (perhaps from way back) and certain situations trigger it to explode.

It's confusing when suddenly you think that you're not good enough. My Bad Bitch felt this way when she was being slain by her own nastiness, which was piggybacked with bad wishes from others. It wasn't that she wasn't good enough, it was that she was too good to keep going in the wrong direction, so she was detoured. Still, there came a time when this implant needed to be removed because not being good enough is not good enough.

Consider how babies are such pure beings that it's not in their nature to ever feel not good enough because we don't come in that way. We come into this world in a wondrous state that eventually gets kiboshed by opinions and false explanations. Another implant is: *This won't work*, a secret kamikaze bomb that sabotages everything we do. Or maybe the thought that: *We're too old, too young, too stupid,* or *too weak* to get anything done. How about: *You can't be successful, you don't fit the format, your work is not good,* or *you don't deserve!* These thoughts are all implants and like an addict shooting

intravenously, we buy into some crappy belief system and poison ourselves with it. Stepping into our power, we clear our psyche and rise above these instilled self-doubts, as our worthiness removes them from our consciousness.

The antidotes are: *Don't go to the polluted well to drink. Drop the friends who pass the poison. Change the dynamic around innuendo. Empower your beliefs.* The worst implant is: *The world is fu*ked.* We think the problems are too huge, the corruptions too powerful, so we give up. This is social conditioning, the wave that makes us feel hopeless. This conditioned energy field wants to tire us out, so we yield. When this happens it's best to shut down this kind of conditioning by staying open to our passion. Know that when what's going on becomes too much, it snaps us out of our numbness and we suddenly find ourselves protesting in the streets. Bravo, we're back! We've removed some big, heavy, jailing, implants by not feeding them. As our passion towards things gives us the pull that will override all implants and restore us.

In order to remove an implant, we must define it. The symptoms are: We're feeling off kilter, things are not flowing; we keep getting rejections, there are constant delays, we repeatedly question ourselves and don't feel like we're on the right path. What's happening is that these offsetting times are bringing things to the surface and by knowing what the exact issues are that knock us off our power place, we focus on them to transform them. One of mine is that someone has put a curse on my business when it's not

sparking. This is total bullshit. I put a curse on it by believing that story and in seeing this I quickly remove the curse. The rejections are blessings that we are in the wrong situations, the delays are periods to ramp up our magic and feeling lost leads to finding our way.

One morning I woke up while on a juice cleanse, shaken by feelings of impending doom from dark dreams. I thought: *Oh no, here comes another shit storm* and *of course I deserve it.* I then went to write my Artist Way morning pages (a writing exercise using stream of consciousness) and was in a poor-me zone, when a voice from some other dimension yelled out, "*Hell No!*" I quickly woke up (even though I was technically awake) to understand that while I'm in the midst of a physical cleanse, of course old emotional crap will come up to be released. Interesting that as I was writing about implants, they surfaced. I wondered if they heard me and thought I was calling them? I then realized that implants are not very smart, and they don't have their own consciousness, so they have to use ours—and when we change ours, they weaken.

Energy attracts like-kind energy, so as I thought about releasing implants, antidotes surfaced. I heard voices telling me what to do. One said: *Write a letter to yourself from your higher self.* I did, and the instructions said: *Be serious around this cleanse, you are healing lifetimes of old paradigms that you've carried. Treat this release as a ceremony and take three days to remove these old implants.* From this moment, every dark

emotion I'd ever felt came up for clearing. I was literally nauseous. It felt like I was puking fears and old stinking thinking down a cosmic drain. I did not try to stop the outflow, but just witnessed it and when it got worse, I questioned if it would ever end. A voice said, *Hang in there.* Suddenly, I felt elated even while the same craziness was still ongoing. The voice said: *Don't look at the craziness!* I then heard: *This is not your craziness; you are changing patterns and are now in your best archetype–stay there!* The barrage ended, and I was left clearly open to possibility and empowered to hold a new state of being.

The message is that every time we catch ourselves getting pulled into a deceptive stream of consciousness, it's a sign that we need to counterbalance. Granted, we can't walk around in space suits to protect ourselves from all that is constantly flying around, though instead of getting hysterical (feeding the negative) just turn it around to see what the setup is and then rearrange it. Our ego will say one thing and maybe we'll spend years on its high horse, until the day our horse collapses under our kinetic weight load. This happens because we're no longer getting away without soul-searching for where our bounty is. It's time to take a hard look deep inside ourselves; own what we see, then stand in our highest power around our lowest vibrations and pull up all the bullshit we've bought into–it could get ugly. So we reach into our consciousness and pull out false concepts, negativity, antagonizing emotions, and dispirited roots that are embedded, and in doing so we spotlight these adversities! Next, dislocate, drag, and yank them from your

actuality until you feel free of them.

It's hardest for people who can't be wrong, the perfectionists who give a million excuses for why they have to do it their way. This is a time to be wrong, be totally wrong and agree to learn from mistakes. When our afflictions are guarding our ego-gate, saying things like: *how dare they* and *this isn't right*, we're shutting down doing the excavation of seeing what we hold on to that's hurting more than supporting us. Maybe *how dare they* is true, but going deeper, it's about *how dare I* allow this kind of crap to ever continue. The question being is: What is it inside us that thinks we're right, while in the midst of a turmoil that really isn't right? Think about it.

Right now we're all in the midst of an energetic cleanse where we are being supported to elevate and release all that's not good enough. I imagine my afflictions as daggers that I remove and throw into the sun to be burnt to smithereens. After these energetic evictions, I sit quietly to see who I am without them. Once we see ourselves as liberated, we must seal this vision in. We might have to do this a few times, maybe often, but it's no big deal, it's like brushing our teeth. Every day, we simply strip-search ourselves for entities, negative implants, and dark thoughts—and we remove them. Conviction is our wand here.

We've all arrived for this Earth journey with an innate bag of treasures; if we got robbed of them during childhood it's time to retrieve them now. We did not come here to be lost in muck. We came to dream and be part of the magic

that we are. This is the shift that's happening now, so if you feel like you're spinning you actually are. You're in the cosmic washing machine clearing away all that you don't need. You might lose friends, houses, things, jobs, but you won't lose your magic, in fact it's more enhanced because now there's space for it. When the clearing is intense, just stay with it so it moves faster. Don't try to grab things back as they roll by, let them all go as they move out. And don't take it personally or feel bad about your negative attributes either because it's a human condition to step in shit, just wash it off. Last, when you get to a place of unknowing, then know you've come clean, as the mystery is where the magic exists and begins!

Most importantly, be clear about what your soul direction is because implants want to confuse us. A woman who decided to sell her house and drive across America was one-pointed until everyone around her threw their agendas into her pot. All those agendas were implants, so the woman began to falter on her dream. I had gotten her an offer that was a miracle when she decided she didn't like the buyer and suddenly she could not sell him her house. The ego is a big implant that lies, twists things around and makes us believe it's right. I was stunned that she went so far off track as to lose sight of her dream. In the end, knowing the deal would be a blessing, I brought her and her buyer together on a conference call and held heart energy for them both. It worked, and the deal went through all because one of the parties (being me) broke down the false assumptions they

had about each other.

A young woman working in my local health food store just got her citizenship to live in Italy. She manifested step one of her dream, though when I asked her when she would move there, she seemed lost and looked at me for an answer. "I don't know what I would do there," she said. I suggested that she make something up and watched her wheels spin over the possibility that she was free to do just that. How often do we hook into our ability to play with ideas, to open our treasure chest, peruse our gifts, dream of something that makes our pulse race? We must, but first we have to wake up, emerge from the poppy field, and throw a bucket of water on our wicked witch to calm her down. Then we can become a team spirit with all aspects of ourselves and disarm the implants (the flying monkeys). Once we charge up our ruby slippers, we can walk anywhere in them without being fazed, even through energetic minefields.

We become the wizard, the alchemist and the diviner, as we entice our enlightened charms to come into focus on the sage path of good faith. Here, the hidden treasures are exposed to us, so we can blow them into proportion. In these days of transformation, our Yellow Brick Road is about cleaning up and weaving gold out of any shit we might have stepped in or had flung at us. Again, conviction is our wand.

In the early days of the Coronavirus Pandemic, I had a real estate deal that was going bad with a lowly buyer and a hysterical seller who'd already emptied out her house and moved away based on a scheduled closing two days later. The

closing never happened. The buyer continued to jerk this seller down for money as he had the sale locked up by a contract he would not release, so the seller could not even sell to someone else. I felt an implant of rage for the indecency of this buyer, it then became clear that this was a karmic predicament between the parties that had nothing to do with me. Meanwhile our world was in a tornado of fear around the pandemic and the tragic loss of life, so I stepped back to clear my energy field. It was a question of where my vitality was present, and I got the clear message that it wasn't vital that I be in the middle of someone else's karma. Once we define where it's best to be involved, our vibration begins to resonate more highly, then what's going on will either connect in with our higher vibration or not, while all else is up for clearing. The deal with the buyer finally closed, as when I raised my energy, the lower energy that was stuck moved to meet us all on my higher level. Though I was prepared to lose that deal and wait for the next one, it was my belief in the bigger picture that shifted the energy.

The Coronavirus crisis brought out the worst in some people and the best in others. It's like a full moon amplifying what already existed but was hidden. Every time a new layer of fear and anxiety arose, I considered it there for clearing. At the same time, while our poor quality of life was being dynamically cleared out, the air was clearing and pollution was lowered, while many beings left this planet to support us from the other side. Recovering from shock we tried to make the best of it while we battled anxiety, fear, depression, and

illness. Our hearts broke on a daily basis as there was no room for what was less than love, so people dropped their shit and behaved kindly to each other. In quarantine, we became stronger, more solidified in our ideas, closer to spirit, more open, and more united with each other—all without ever touching. We got it that we're all in this crisis together and we're all clearing a new way.

Clearing Unfavorable Implants . . .

- A yoga teacher I once practiced with always spoke about her wound of not being enough, which was surprising because she seemed to have everything going on. The first step to being enough is owning that you are and not talking otherwise. We must let those false thoughts go, as they don't belong in our light field.
- Define the beliefs, the blocks, and the distortions that you're carrying. Write about them. Be honest, be raw, and be real. Once you have a list of these paradoxes, burn them. Next, seal the wounded spaces where they existed with self-love and leave it be. Can it be this easy? It can if we believe it to be.
- Once you've defined the implants, act otherwise from them. "*Acting as If*" sets the stage for our new productions. This reminds me of the time when I had broken beliefs and was literally broke. Affirming that I was a money-magnet—I shortly become one.

- What to do when someone who doesn't believe in you and triggers a wound? Talk to the wound, tell it you have it covered so it can bleed out its old story and heal.
- Acknowledge that when a wound is triggered it's being held by an implant and remove it.
- Ego will reason and battle for its premise, so recognize the battle as egoic bravado and move beyond it. Getting to the source of truth is worth battling for.
- Tap into your supreme nature and dwell there.
- Our essential attributes spotlight and reconcile false myths.
- Replace past implants with charmed visions and affirm them.
- Don't hang out in frequencies you've outgrown.
- Mind power acts as a shield against habitual skepticism.
- Always hold an air of expectancy.
- Intentions targeted toward evolution are charged by the universe.
- Do a daily cleanse of implants.
- Be aware of uncomfortable feelings and address them, as: "*Is this thought true, or is this a negative implant?*" If you find an implant, mentally abolish its energy field. Come up with imaginative ways; like my example of an etheric vacuum cleaner that sucks up negativity and delivers it into the sun to burn up.

- Without implants, we come into balance.
- Hold high frequencies.
- If the implants are deep-seated, we might have to do a twenty-one day fast on them. This means deliberately focusing on disbelieving all misrepresentation that we have invested in.
- It's important not to talk about removing implants while doing it. The more we share our displaced feelings, the more we're empowering them and giving them energy. The feelings that want to own us lose all power when we replace them with new impressions.
- Stop describing what's wrong and start talking about what's right.
- When in a disagreement where you're being judged or called names, know that the other party is describing themselves and giving insight into who they are.
- Ignore the labels, the opinions, and expectations of others.
- Awareness is an entity of its own that stands at our gate to guard what is allowed to enter.
- There's no juju out there stronger than the power of our own considerations.
- People can wish us ill, judge us and be jealous, but this is all innuendo that should not be touched or even reckoned with.
- Mastery over ego brings higher order.

- As we elevate ourselves, we're removed from dark energy fields and cannot be reached.
- Instead of retaliation, stay in your bliss.
- Exhilaration lifts us off shadow frequencies.
- When disturbing things come up to be healed–heal them.
- Focus on what is calling for love and send love.
- Send love to your anger, your disappointments and your defense modes.
- Love loosens implants, so send them love as you remove them.
- Always ask for divine assistance.

MANIFESTING ABUNDANCE
Materializing in Motion

"Our ideas come when we least expect them. They come in the night when we can't sleep, in the shower, in our dreams, and in memories. Arriving from an abundant cosmos when we are open–be open."

We sit around and think and dream of what we want, but how often do we sit waiting for direction? I have spent years placing my orders and dreaming my reality into form and this worked because I was going higher than playing with things like power and maneuvers. My inner bitch cannot not relax, especially when at the top of her game, faced with the threat of constantly being knocked off her pedestal. Holding her position was exhausting and being successful was debilitating due to her distorted state. It was such a never-ending toil that when the checks finally rolled in, I felt like I was bleeding and needed to go to an astral hospital to heal. It was this backbreaking way of doing business that finally led to a burnout and crash. After my recovery, the Good Witch changed all the parameters of how we now go. I find myself in nonstop steadfast training, sitting daily in silence

waiting for direction that always comes while I dream up new ideas. Passion meets me in my conference room where I define my rationale, while, my inner bitch is now calmed down and on CBD oil.

A woman I knew from the past was in tears at our local health food store, telling me how her house was being foreclosed and she didn't have the money to move. Called to help, I found a buyer who'd pay her to leave and buy her house from the bank. As soon as she felt relief, she began acting insane or probably she was insane and it surfaced. She became abusive, blaming, and wanted to cheat me out of being paid while her buyer began to do the same. I had gotten on the crazy bus and knew I had to get off right away and wait for another bus. I stepped away, wished her the best of luck, and left a huge commission on the table because dealing with the energy of this woman was not worth it. When I asked the Universe why I deserved this, I was told: *"The goodness you offer may not pay you back from where you delivered it, but it will pay."* This message literally saved me, as I was ready to shut down all my kind considerations in the future.

Our sustenance might not be coming from where we expect, though if we keep showing up and doing what we do, it always arrives from somewhere. I did find out in the end that her deal did not go through because Ms. Crazy also scared off her buyer. A few weeks later, a new deal came to fruition out of the blue with the kindest buyer and I knew it was my *doing good for others* payback. The message was: You

can't shut down your natural flow of goodness due to bad experiences.

Crappy experiences are not always in our control, but we can file them in the section of what's no longer taking us down and keep going towards the otherwise. The most important action is action, so even when the horizon looks bleak, we start planting seeds. First, we plant them wherever we go, and then we nurture what nurtures us. Second, we don't hold onto the fact that things didn't work, instead we work with what the Universe has to offer.

In turmoil, my inner bitch who is carrying a suitcase full of wounds is on a bullhorn screaming about what's wrong, while the light and lively Good Witch with zero baggage is down the road quietly scouting what's next. Bad Bitch is shrieking that we need money, while Good Witch drives her magical Mercedes away into the create-a-sphere, a mystical zone riddled with new resources. Minutes later, Good Witch circles around and pulls Bad Bitch into the car and gives her a list of what's now on the agenda. It's time to get to work, action phase, which means: Send out the letters and queries, book the appointments, write the book, make a hundred calls, show up on go-sees, manufacture the piece, fill out the application, sign up for the class, take the next client, apply for the job, just do something! Taking action is treading into the flow of manifestations where it's all already happening.

We all want more! More love, more happiness, good health, more energy, and enough money. But how often do we want to give more? The mind will always come up with

the why and how of things, as it abhors doing things in new ways and prides itself on being right. My nasty inner bitch's mentality is *Me First*. Good Witch, on the other hand, knows that in order to receive we must give. In the immortal words of Gandhi, "*Be the change you wish to see in the world.*" If we want more love, more money, more consideration, we must imbibe more of these things in spirit and offer them out.

I wanted to get my *Abracadabra* books into my favorite shop in Manhattan and I did. It's called The Alchemist's Kitchen, and while in a meeting with the owner, he asked me how I planned to create abundance around my books. I hadn't intellectually gotten to that point as I'd been consumed with the creation process. Realizing that my next step was about how the energy exchange of my work would support me, I considered what I'd do to support it. First, I had to stop doing what wasn't supporting me, which meant it was time to be picky about where I invest my energy. Second, I had to start spending money; I needed to invest in my work and lavish time on it. I was being called to believe in my project beyond any doubt. Passion does this to us, it doesn't sit around but grabs us and is always asking: *What more can we give to what we love?*

We must also treat ourselves with love and respect and not go where it's not. A woman I sold a house to wanted to become my real estate partner, it shortly became revealing that she had quite a huffy side. Her first blow-up was when I recommended her a worker that she requested for her own house and the worker never showed up. This woman blew a

fuse and I knew I could never work with her. She quickly apologized, and I thought to perhaps forgive her outburst. A week later she texted me a lowing-up angry head emoji over another mishap and then said that was a mistake. In my world there are no mistakes, as while this woman was ranting at me over the phone, quite suddenly my phone died and disconnected her. I love when the Universe gets involved and saves me.

The message is to follow the signs, as abundance has plans for us and self-respect is the first order. Every time things don't work out, it means stuff is being rearranged to create space, because abundance needs space to grow. Consider that when nothing is happening, especially during the excruciating in-betweens; we must still hold a good state while the winds of change are blowing so something new can come to be. Even when things don't work out, our delving into a perspective around higher reasoning is a form of thriving that calls for bounty and so we must define the abundance we need and own it. I asked a friend who was in manifesting mode to define exactly what she wanted and to write it down and then be thankful for receiving it prior to its arrival.

Good fortune is a team player that flourishes in potent mind-sets prior to bearing fruit. Our fortune may be hiding in the actuality of all that's going on, even in what looks bleak or is a squabble. Everything is a stepping-stone, so address all issues even if only to release them. We're being called to liberate our stinking thinking, our failure to create,

our inability to change, our lack of financial prosperity, our incapacity to receive love, and our attachments to annoying people who are not an asset. We can't sit around describing how bad things are, waiting to be saved. Instead define the change needed, then converse with it, listen to its directive and honor it. Don't be scared of what it takes to create emancipation from limitations, even as the force of change is pushing us over the brink. When we're going over the edge, we're held close by cosmic forces, even more so than when maneuvering on solid ground and especially while our soul is creating our new reality,

I agreed to help an old friend sell his building in Manhattan and it became apparent that even though he wanted a better life, he could not let go of his old one. We brought him offers and when we finally found the perfect buyer, he unexpectedly took the listing off the market. He wasn't ready. My city business partner had walked away after the first meeting with him, saying she had no time to waste with someone who was not realistic. I wanted to fix her wrong assessment of him and learned that when we're constantly trying to fix things in other people, we're wasting time. She was right, time and energy are valid, and we must look at how we give it away and for what reason. I find that being unrealistic has an advantage that defines where we're at, because we might really be more realistic than the reality that's running.

In general, we have to get on the straightforward path with ourselves. Here we walk differently and maybe in reality our ruby slippers are Prada combat boots, since in the

modern world we're going into action. Go for the boots, the love, the money, the happiness, and more. Also go for the fact that if we have to pull over while nothing is going on, we still won't accept what's less-than and will stand firm in our good spirit until something shows up to inspire us. Our pot of gold might not be immediately at hand, but it does exist, and when we clear our blocked energy, the way to it is accessible. We don't have to capture the pot of gold; we just need to get into the head-space of where it exists and partake of its energy field—for us to be shown us how to retrieve it.

The plan is to dream up our bountifulness on the cosmic plane. We're allowed to let loose on imagining what we fancy (valid or not) and play with reveries. Our energy is valuable and aligning it with prosperity makes it want to deliver. Though since the creation void is always in the process of manifesting something, patience around timing is respect for growth. When the action called for is to pull back and spend time in our create-a-sphere, it's not a waste of time, as our abundance flourishes when we energize it to do so. As such we dream up our bed of roses and connect with it on the cosmic plane. We then take action by putting creative energy into plenitude and pulling our lifeforce away from all that drains it.

The purposeful act of un-manifesting all negative thought forms we have put into creation is the final power-play. Examples: "*The world can't support this, it won't work, I'm not good enough!*" Or how about: "*Others are better than me, this world is so screwed, nothing I do matters, I'm a loser, a has-been, too*

wounded. I'm hexed, my party is over. I'm too old, too fat, too ugly, too stupid!" These are all mental implants and we need to replace these lowly thoughts along with any poor-me stories, even if they have justifications, because all they do is keep us in a stronghold.

I used to think *Just Dump the Dreck.* Now I feel it's best to replace what doesn't work with what I want to manifest. So, insert, override, enforce, and sanction the opposite of your shadowed thoughts by believing otherwise. Be thankful for what's going on, take every lousy experience and find the gold in it. Yes, you heard right: even if you feel like vomiting over the shitty experience. Ok, it's true it was probably shitty, but once we find our enlightenment through it, we're back on our way. Replace your negatives with: "*I'm blessed, I'm a success, I'm wealthy, I'm healed, I attract abundance, I am beautiful, I'm loved, the Universe is on my side, my abundance is happening now!*" Taking on our power, we no longer rely on the outside world to boost our juice and we don't wait for people to love us back to life. We're doing it for ourselves!

My grandmother was a great witch in her time; she manifested millions of dollars during an era when it was unheard of to make this kind of money. Grandma Sally came from the wrong side of the tracks and illegitimately gave birth to my father. Back in those days, being a never-wed single mother was considered shameful. All the odds were against her, but she couldn't care less what the running ideology was because she believed that she was someone of value. Sally eventually married Marty, who worked in his family's rubber

fabrics company. He adopted my father and with few resources they struggled. Grandma Sally was not a beauty per se, but she thought she was and had vixen energy. Sally took the foam rubber from the vats at her husband's factory and stuffed her bra with it to achieve a Jane Russell movie-star look.

One day, Sally asked my Grandfather to design a half-moon piece of foam covered in silk to uplift her assets, so to speak. She patented this bra foam and sold it to all the great designers of the day. She then sold her bra foam, known as: "*Falsies*" to a bra manufacturing company for millions of dollars. *Voila!* Sally hit her Lotto and rolled right into the grand birthright she believed she should have all along.

Interestingly, my grandmother's inner bitch was the guard who protected her Good Witch aspects, so no one could ever get over on her. Her Bad Bitch had balls and was brash with a mouth like a truck driver, while her Goddess side was kind and giving–she was in balance with herself. My mother said Sally had no class, but she was in a class of her own. She was uncensored and held her ground. Her Bad Bitch stood at her gate, yelling at idiots to get the fu*k out and they did. That was the worst of it, as Sally was not one to annihilate others. She never needed to be manipulative or act like a bitch, for she was too busy manifesting what she wanted. The thing about Grandma Sally was that she solidly inhabited her reality, which revolved around all the things she believed she deserved, and the Universe met her on her dance floor and delivered.

Our manifesting partner is faith inspired by passion, and

when we find these two, we're good to go. Walking on the beach one day, I pulled my scarf out of my pocket and a penny fell to the sand. I heard a strong message inside that said, "*Leave it there.*" Further on, I found a quarter in the sand and mind you, I've never found money on the beach and knew this was a message from the Universe saying; "*More is here.*" Oftentimes when I'm working on manifesting more finances, I leave a dollar on a bench, or on a taxi seat. I give money to the homeless and I feed stray cats. We must remember to offer out what we want to return to us. So, if it's love we seek, we must be loving. If forgiveness is desired, we must be forgiving. If our creativity yearns to manifest, then we must support the creativity of others.

Our manifestations are tapped into the spinning of our magic in motion; we are energetically spinning like whirling dervishes on a planet that's also spinning, as we whirl in our visions. It's time to envision being our own essential advisor, art director, healer, hero, Guru, and Godsend. We're our own everything that's connected to the Divine Spirit of the great all-there-is. Therefore, sit with yourself, establish your production, author the book, give birth to the dream, and honor your passion as the guide to where you're going. Also remember that you're manifesting more than just things, you're manifesting the reasoning behind things. Once we define our premise, then everything our reasoning needs for our materializing to become established is set forth. I always imagine that I'm on my way to the premiere of my next creation and the excitement I feel on my way fuels me.

I never wanted to sell real estate and I never wanted to be involved in a corporate business model, as I was always a bohemian artist type–more like a dreamy hippie. I loved yard sales and looking at houses and envisioned owning each one I visited. I loved houses because I needed to nest in order to manifest my soul assignment even though I had no idea what that was, it was just a feeling. The next thing I find is that I'm drawn into real estate as a top producer! Abundance that manifests from passion is a God Source of wealth. It's about paying attention to what's needed, seeing what resonates highest in a situation, finding how we can be part of it all and offering it out. During the Coronavirus quarantine, it became obvious that every time I hooked into the news, I became depleted and depressed. Being cataclysmic from the shock, the time called for a higher understanding of the magnanimous changes needed. I innately knew that this was a time of darkness coming into the light and that I had to quarantine myself from fear and low-level thinking to get through it.

I have to go on constant personal retreats to retrieve myself. I'm dedicated to shifting my reality higher and I do this from home. I have pure intentions about what I request to happen and mostly have no idea what will transpire, though I'm creating a platform for it to arrive. A friend who happened to be visiting me while I was on one of my retreats said her inner Good Witch was also sparked by this activity. She'd been stuck in a slump but put her blight aside when she spent time with me. A stimulus was transmitted since my energy field had ignited my passion and was materializing

bounty onto everything and everyone around me. My friend described welcoming herself back home as she clearly remembered a most powerful prior aspect of herself. Materializing in motion happens on the inside first and then sparks us back to life, as it abundantly charges everything up.

Materializing in Motion

- I create as I speak that________________________. Add the desire in the blank and repeat it constantly as a mantra.
- Do not invest energy or continue to talk about what you don't want.
- Good will overrides bad feelings.
- Intentions are more powerful than anxiety—empower your intentions every time you feel anxiety.
- Sometimes a retreat is necessary to clear the slate. A day will do it, though a week really is amazing. Clear your energy during this time and stay open to a higher cosmic plan.
- Be open to receive, keep your disposition light, and hold joy.
- A spark of insight, a bolt of passion, a vision of inspiration, needs to be followed boldly.
- Inform your heart what you're invested in and that you're not empowering otherwise.
- Every time the otherwise shows up, switch channels to your new station.

- Define your reasoning, as a high rationale empowers our manifestations.
- Always say what you wish to establish as if it's already been manifested.
- Celebrate your success every day for the more we celebrate the more we attract.
- Own your abundance, breathe it, taste it, live it in your mind as if it were real.
- Believe in yourself! Write: ***I Believe in Myself.*** Write it over and over until it clicks in.
- Manifestations are alive first in a quantum field, while their physical forms are being established. Instill good vibes to birth your demonstration.
- Positive-minded thought sanctions abundance.
- During difficult times, hold strong to your motives.
- Make an imagination board—make many of them.
- Write your manifestations on notes, candles, in sand at the beach, in chalk at the park; spark them often to keep them alive.
- Affirm to yourself that your manifestation is happening now.
- Be careful that what you ask for is fueled only by love, not by emotions or anger.
- A recommitment strengthens intention.
- Love, kindness, and understanding will manifest abundance and clear karma.
- Prayers and good wishes for others come back to us.
- New ideas are ethereal guidance—follow them.

- Always be open to signs and gifts along the way—and be ready to change directions.
- Share whatever you have to keep your financial current moving.
- Don't hoard unnecessary stuff.
- Don't spend time fearing loss; instead, use your energy to create more grace.
- Love yourself so you'll be a perfect match for Universal Love.
- Remember, we're not manifesting alone, we're always in partnership with Divine Spirit.
- Say *Thank You* before and after every manifesting expression.
- *Thank You, Thank You, Thank You!* This seals our appeal.
- When struggles are happening, see them as lessons so you can find the gold in them.
- Expect Miracles.
- Sometimes odd things show up—honor them as part of the miracle.
- Once we've gotten the lesson, we find the gold.
- Never take anything for granted—always see everything as a gift from the Universe.
- Be in your greatness, stand in your dream, and relish it.
- We are visionaries who manifest by believing in our visions.
- We are our own heroes, so act as one.

- Treasure yourself, treasure exactly where you are, and treasure what you already have, as gratitude attracts and multiplies riches.
- Good will is the bridge to our abundance—the bridge is made out of esteem, benediction, and grace—and right now we're standing on it. Amen!

KARMA CLEANSE
Converting Sh*t To Gold

"There are no mistakes, every meeting of chance is karma, every experience is part of it. When we find gold in the dung pile, we have converted bad karma to grace."

I have always believed in reincarnation, past lives, and multidimensional realities. I have proof of these things from experiences that cannot be denied, including a near-death experience where I saw that this life was not the only reality. I know there is an afterlife because I'm always meeting people whom I innately feel I've traveled with before. It's when you meet someone who you feel like you've known all your life and believe me you have. And then there are those annoying people in our lives that we are stuck with. We even love them at times, though dealing with them is a full-on challenge because these are the ones that we're burning karma with. You know them because you wish you didn't, you can't get rid of them, and they drive you crazy. Make a list of these bothersome folks and crown them as great teachers.

This lifetime, along with every other lifetime we've had, is our opportunity to learn the hard way and wipe our karmic slates. We all know a few unconscious souls and it's shocking to say that at one time or other, we've all been them. We've all made mistakes. Some of us have committed horrible things, atrocities, and have been downright evil. Even though it's hard to comprehend, consider that this evil isn't the essence of our soul, but of a lost being playing with darkness. Our mistakes feel shameful, searing us with a curse that we need to clear along with the karma attached to it. In human-ness, we are many times lost or busy following the flock, while our Great Spirit is banging on our doors trying to wake us up. Suddenly a delivery of great struggle arrives, and we slam the door shut. Ding-dong, it's most probably a karmic teaching that is not going away until we get it. Great Spirit is saying, *"Forget the struggle, get the teaching and you are done with this."*

When I was mostly a nasty bitch, I was into revenge. When someone hurt me, I wished them hellish thoughts. I was playing in the ring with deceitful, untrustworthy people and took their betrayals personally. By constantly attracting a Judas dynamic from my ill will, even though I knew better, I was creating more bad karma. I had read all the books, even wrote some books, but it wasn't till it hit me that retaliation boomerangs the same shit back to us. I got the memo that my nasty bitch was a bad karma magnet. When bad things happened, I always asked, "Is this my bad karma?" My husband would say, "No, this is the way people are." I was right to ask that question, as people can be self-serving,

greedy, needy, pains in the ass, and since these behaviors affected me, I had karma around them.

Another karmic story involves a loved one who was doing drugs, and instead of having compassion for her pain, I was judging and doing battle with her to get her to stop. This relationship tortured me my entire life but was not one I could walk away from and I tried many times. This woman was my mother, a great teacher who, when she finally left this world on a cloud of morphine, had bestowed a wake-up call upon me. My anger toward her stemmed from love, I loved her. She taught me that love is greater than every hellish story that has ever happened, for even within our searing grief, love arises and is available. Once I allowed the love to engulf me, I howled for months over her loss, and then one day all that was left was love and the karma was done—it did its job.

As far as past lifetimes go, our karma from back then still bleeds over into the here and now. I believe that when we're done with a lifetime, we come to terms with it. Dropping our human-ness, we come into a soul perspective and can see the elevated story. We learn the lessons, but still there is clean-up to be done. So, we come back to clear the decks, or maybe we arrive for the benefit of someone else, perhaps to accompany them through a rough lifetime. We help others because we've evolved, becoming enlightened enough from every past experience to offer others liberation by example. If you're not sure what you're doing here, think about who your presence benefits or what your existence is offering to

the greater whole. It could be something like you rescue animals, because in a past life you'd slain them. Maybe you're an advocate for good causes or a secret saint that got lost in a mind shuffle and you're back.

We all have a saint hanging out in our temple and when we get Holy with them, they walk out in front of us to pave our way. In point, we can evolve radically in this exact lifetime, as when I put my nasty bitch to bed, my Good Witch stepped in to cleanse karma from many past lifetimes. The shift was that I stopped feeding the fire of anger, revenge, and fear, instead endeavoring to stoke the embers of Love. We must love ourselves first in order to share it, as we can't give what we don't have, and we can't attract what is not in our frequency. This does not mean that we now have to sit down and break bread with the people who do not wish us well–it means we let it go.

Alarms are going off, hearts are banging out a war song, a veil of rage has covered our eyes, and at times we've lost ourselves to hatred. It bleeds into all our cells and the next thing we know is that our life force has left us in a puddle on the floor. A shadow of depression arrives to smother us in its lust and insane voices come online instilling hopelessness by telling us: *We deserve it!* We try to disconnect from the voices, but they won't shut up, and they affect us even when we know they're full of it. There are no words for how hard it is to wrestle ourselves into love when despicable waves of desolation show up. If we're lucky enough to have done prior karmic work, we will see this as a passing wave, though

it's really a reminder telling us that there's still umbrage that needs to be dismantled in our psyche. Sorry to say, there's no way out but through—and in the aftermath, many pieces come together as our realizations wake us up to enlighten us.

I felt slayed when I reached out to my old best friend from decades ago, who wasn't talking to me. I put my hand out and my heart on the table to offer love and healing. She ignored my offering and blocked me on social media. In the past, we'd both spent time at the feet of a guru who taught about higher consciousness, well so much for that! You can get conscious and drop it in an emotional minute when a wound grabs you. In that moment, I felt bad about myself, like I was a hideous person for being such a bitch back in the day. I figured I deserved to be rejected. False! People close to me who knew my old friend felt otherwise, declaring that she was the one not behaving well in the here and now.

One friend told me that when I was a hideous bitch, that they saw it was coming from a severe trauma that I was protecting myself from. They witnessed me devoted to myself as a warrior and said there was never a time I was more honest. I was like the Goddess Durga, who had multiple arms and rode a tiger: she was a warrior who rolled through conflict-ridden dramas to conquer low-level consciousness. This concept healed me. I no longer felt a need to make peace with my old friend. I also came to understand that karma is a gift of lessons, and that the struggle and pain of it lies in our resistance to master the teachings. Letting go is one of the most profound lessons, for as we cling to old

concepts, past regrets, and a lack of self-love—we're in pain. Letting go is an undoing of mistrust and judgements that lead to liberation and dissolve negative karma.

Immersed in doing a life dance of fall-down/get-up, we see that none of what's going on is personal, and that the only thing personal is the conversation we're having with ourselves and how lost we become in our slip-slides. When the bombs go off on our inner inferno, the trick is to use this blaze to burn karma. The burning of karma is triggered by a bonfire in our soul that devours our wrong considerations. What has already gone amiss needn't be argued, but caring about it can be diversified, especially when it has gone to the point of taking us down.

My bitch is a confronter with a get-up-in-your-face persona and not one who can sit in discomfort. She has thus caused much unnecessary karma for herself though her bigmouth actions. The Good Witch, on the other hand, knows how to sit in discomfort and disseminate it by un-investing in what the squeeze is because her mantra is: *It's not worth it!* The quick fix that dismantles squirming discomfort is when we remember to reach beyond ourselves to our Divine Spirit's light-filled arena. Once we're tapped into this lit frequency, a lesson is spotlighted—and once we get the lesson, the karma is disseminated.

A woman that I considered a friend and trusted, after a decade of on-and-off renting and listing her house for sale, did not pay me on a property that I had hammered away at selling. Supposedly, a buyer contacted her directly—probably

one I procured from the long list of showings I had done. My friend told me not to worry, that I could trust her even though she was now going to do the deal herself, and that she would pay me. In the end, she paid me a quarter of what was due and sent a note saying I was lucky she paid me at all, since our contract had expired, and she legally owed me nothing. Wow! I argued this discrepancy, but technically she was right: the contract on paper had expired, so I was working on trust and got screwed. What I felt about this woman haunted me, and even though I knew the remedy was to send love anyway, I could not get to it.

One evening, months later, I experienced severe emotions around this event and couldn't get it out of my mind. I often had to drive by her old house, which would trigger my Bad Bitch to get her middle finger up, even though I knew better. On this evening of turmoil, the event became like an entity that broke into my house and opened all my drawers, knocking things over and making a mess. I tried many distractions, such as spending an hour on Instagram, which worked until the entity-like feelings popped in again and I would relive the experience. It's funny how the Universe gets in on the game. The next morning while reading the local news, there she was with blaring bravado, praised for buying an expensive new home. This home was named after a witch, as it had a pointy tower. Bells went off, and I knew I could get to the needed remedy, because now the Universe was directly talking to me, saying, "*Put on your Good Witch hat!*"

The remedy was to send love and blessings to this woman.

I knew I had to do it to clear the karma, even though I didn't feel any love for her at all. I sat and pulled up good wishes and threw childlike love bombs in her direction. As I played with this light-filled energy, I realized she was a teacher who, through her shitty actions, pushed me to a higher plateau. I asked myself if, in the long run, it was worth it to be more of the kind of person who was not carrying bags of hate. It was. So, I sat and sent more love and blessings until I felt the karma with her was done. The clearing went beyond this one experience to cover the many times that ugliness and greed in the real estate industry got to me. My ability to trust had been tampered with, but it neutralized when I decided I was not a victim, just sometimes an idiot who trusted blindly. I learned that discrimination was called for and to always get the paperwork signed—even with friends.

Once we identify our spiritual go-between, we're banded like the spokes connected to a wheel ready to roll. The more we honor the connection, the more freely the wheel rolls. Granted, we will come to surrender folks who are not on our wavelength, patterns that drag us down, bad attitudes and wounds—though we will be so satiated with new rectitude that we won't miss any of it. When we accept the fact that bad things happened, people left, we were not treated well, and on it goes, we must find some meaning in it all that we can live with, which releases us from Hell. And, as far as the people we leave behind goes we wish them to be blessed, to be happy and loved, for what we wish for others is exactly what we attract.

When we lost my niece Kenza to an overdose of some drug laced with Fentanyl, we wanted to know who sold it to her. In her phone was a text from another kid, who said he tried to wake her up but couldn't. He then put a pillow under her head, borrowed twenty dollars from her wallet to get home, and left. He could have saved her life, but it didn't happen that way. The police detectives did track him down and were going to go after him, as my brother and my family were on a warpath to blame someone.

At Kenza's funeral, there were a few hundred people; she was so loved. One young blond boy stood out, for he was visibly a total wreck. Crying and shaking, he approached my brother after the service and said he was so sorry. My brother intuitively knew this boy was the one who'd written the text. He didn't accuse the boy but told him if he needed help to call him. It was a huge surrender of forgiveness when my brother told the police that he did not want to go further in knowing who sold her the drugs, or getting that person put away. He knew who it was and saw that this childlike boy was suffering greatly and that his karma had him. Our girl was gone and all we had left was love in the midst of our pain. The love was a gift from her.

Our karma is not a victim sentence; it's us taking responsibility for our actions and the way we've rolled. There's a choice, and we don't make the higher one because we're scared of a karma payback, we make it because we've learned from our actions. Not everything that happens is our personal fault; consider the inheritance of world karma,

ecological destruction due to past inconsideration, or family karma. We didn't create it, but by being here, we're involved in what exists and even though we're part of an experience that we might not have personally contributed to, it's still our karma to clean it up. Karma questions what we do with turbulence; how we heal it and react to it, not just for ourselves but for the world.

As COVID-19 spread across the planet, it was obvious that we were in the fire of a world karma event. Shortly before, there had been many cataclysmic environmental events: fires, mud slides, earthquakes. Now, we have faced a pandemic that isolated everyone, locking us in our homes while friends and family died. People scrambled to buy provisions, some were in denial, others hoarded items. Many ran to the front lines to help, while we all were forced to come to terms with the loss of a normal way of life, lasting probably forever. On Easter Sunday, in the midst of this crisis, a friend passed on; she'd been battling cancer for six years. This woman was a fighter, always smiling and happy—she was so good-spirited. Most important, she was grateful for every day, though some of her days were beyond uneasy. She was a gift to me, as I needed to own her same demeanor and be grateful every day, especially in the dark of pandemic time.

Appreciating that we're here now, it's our duty and gift as members of the light-body clean-up crew to offer grace to all that's happening, on all planes of existence, every way we can. Stepping into light fields (even imaginary ones) are the recharge zones where we are shredding outmoded paradigms, past

traumas (even worldly ones) and old bullshit. We are in a huge karma cleanse where all the wrongdoings, difficulties, and dark times are coming forth to be purged. Just when we think we've conquered a huge wave of Hell, the next one rolls in and here we are, a team of cleansers restoring the darkness into light as we go. Once we get it that we're here as light-workers, we can still be the CEO, the taxman, the rock star, the police officer, the garbage pickup, and revolutionary people of all colors and sexualities who are morphing into power beings, because beyond all our titles we're huge transformers.

Karma Cleanse

- All negative thoughts boomerang; shut them down and send love.
- Understand that you're in service, so consider *what the Buddha would do* and do that.
- Forgive, Forgive, and Forgive Yourself.
- Make peace and don't indulge further.
- Retribution is none of our business; let the Universe handle it.
- Stay out of other people's shit.
- Don't be needy or leak your issues–it's vampire energy and not healing.
- If your way is not happening, honor that and focus on what is.
- Don't waste energy banging on doors–when one door shuts, find and open another door.

- When people aren't listening, talk to their higher self and let it go.
- Don't indulge in infectious hatred; stay above it.
- Whenever you encounter an *us-and-them* dynamic—focus on sending love to both sides.
- Grief happens in order for us to heal. Remember, you are not sinking—you are healing.
- Healing is sacred acceptance and strength aligned toward rebirth.
- If others send you ill will, the highest form of protection is to send love back.
- If people do shitty things, play with wishing them well until you really can.
- Practice holding compassion for unconsciousness and don't take it personally.
- The more evolved considerations we have, the more liberated we become.
- When bad things happen, hold a witness state, weigh the outcomes then choose the highest one. It might be the hardest task, but it will bring blessings.
- There are times we'll easily succeed and other times where we must struggle to arrive at success; know there are benefits even in the struggle.
- Admit when you're wrong.
- Breaking down self-righteousness acknowledges self-worth.
- Acknowledge that you're aligned with a God force and you are not alone.

- Have humility.
- Always ask for support from the highest source and respectfully do your best.
- The harder the times, the more we are needed as light-workers to balance the darkness.
- Take every opportunity to do good for others.
- Learn from your mistakes and honor the teaching.
- Make amends, and if you can't do it in person, do it in spirit.
- Cherish the knowledge that your Divine Spirit sent you here at this time to help.
- Always be a giver, for it's a gift to support those in need.
- Request directions to connect higher.
- Stay soft, even during hard times.
- Never be afraid to lose what you have: it's all a gift, and there's always more to come.
- Stop resisting and surrender to what's cosmically happening to assist beneficence.
- Once you surrender, you will be given directions.
- We are not here to get lost on this wheel of life, but to become a hub that rolls with it.
- Do no harm, but take no shit, and be kind.
- Always be cleaning, emptying, giving things away.
- Don't be greedy, for it stops the flow and creates greedy karma.
- Keep the focus on what's best.
- Understand impermanence.

- Let go of what has gone or is going and keep the love.
- Keep the reactive mind calm.
- Watch yourself, reflect on your actions, and leave a clean trail.
- Honor what doesn't work and explore what does.
- The highest path goes in all directions; it detours drama and is targeted in love.
- The easy way is not always karmically the highest way.
- Doing the right thing may not be easy, but it will make life easier.
- Be grateful, as gratitude clears karma.
- Don't get lost in what you don't have or what doesn't work—get lost in your passion.
- A confrontation is only a test.
- Outwit your lower self by holding your highest state sacred.
- Raising the vibrations in every instance clears karma.
- Since karma is a teacher, be the student.
- Karma has a consciousness that directs the evolved flow—it slaps you when you don't pay attention, so do pay attention.
- Stay out of other people's drama, but if they ask for help, help them.
- Keep throwing love bombs when you feel like throwing shit.
- When bad things happen, we will go down, but we will get up again—it's our nature.

- Consider the going down as a knee squat, so keep your humor–lighten the way.
- Survival is an entire education in itself.
- Believe in the comeback and come back.

RAISING VIBRATIONS
Elevating Our World

"There is always another avenue to take, it may be a mountain we have to climb. The treasure is not at the end of the road, it's in the journey."

The Debbie Downers are vibrational quicksand, but secretly they're essential, directional guides letting us know where we need to raise our vibrations. As of late, it feels like Armageddon has arrived. Nevertheless, if this is the end-of-the-world party, someone needs to direct traffic. Truly, it's not the end of the world, just the end of how we knew it to be and the beginning of a new world rapidly evolving. Now that we've quaked out of childhood into adolescence and then on into adulthood, someday we will oscillate back into spirit and even come back as a new entity. In the interim, the world can look bleak and scary as non-stop catastrophes rock the planet. Though when Mr. Rogers was terrified as a child from watching the news, his mother told him to look for the helpers, assuring him that he'd always find people who were helping, and this is why he became such a great friend to

children. Like it or not, we're the new helpers, and we came here to serve others.

Up for the challenge? There is no longer a choice, as we're not on stand-by. It's time to honor that we're here in service and our offering is our contribution to raising the world's vibration. This goes for all the interactions we have in our daily life, along with what we spew into the vibratory atmosphere. Someone has pissed me off, crossed a boundary, been selfish, downright annoying and un-evolved. I'm pulled to go at it with them, give them a talking-to, though I grab myself back from indulging, because we don't have to work through everything with others, we just need to raise our vibration. They will either come to meet us on our elevated plateau, or they will go on their way. The new way lies in the fact that we can have a nice chat with someone's higher self, calmly and with love—and then it's out of our hands.

Our service may not be to speak at an environmental conference, or build Habitats for Humanity, or protest inequality, though great if we're pulled to these causes, but it's the bearing we resonate on that matters. Since everything has a reverberation it's about how we hold ourselves and the amicable cadence we bring to the table. Most people don't realize that their personal emotional reactions count and contribute to the balance of order. Yes, one temper tantrum could create a war when the energy field score card becomes dark and heavy. Imagine an ethereal energy bank, and all the good energy is depleted, and we have to put some back in, or we will go broke. This doesn't mean we let things go or look

the other way; it means we show up to transcend anger, fear, and confusion. We speak our truth from a place of power, we control rampant emotions and we commit to our bliss.

Bad Bitch comes from her truth, but her edge had a smacking gleam that caused big trouble, and this was the vibration she rode on, so her offering to the world energy field was chaotic. Once she owned her shit everything shifted and now, she no longer needs to wear an evil eye, but keeps a watchful eye on herself. The mantra for emotional rescue is: "*I am no longer available for the shit that makes me feel bad.*" To own that people will do what they do and that we're responsible for our feelings around it is empowering.

A user client was constantly requesting me to do free work for her and then gave her business to someone else. When I called her to ask about it, she went off on a tangent about how selfish and demanding I was; she was basically describing herself to me. I decided to do self-inquiry on this and saw that Bad Bitch was all these things at times and that's why I attracted this client. Interesting how our past actions always try to sneak back in, so my above mantra is hugely pertinent. Selfish people do what's best for themselves and are low-vibration types, so the trick is to keep raising our vibration anyway, while we wave bye-bye as we ride off on our brooms. It's best to sweep low vibrations out of our consciousness–sometimes on the hour.

As far as sweeping goes, witches and broomsticks evolved around a rumor that women were rubbing a mold fungus that came off rye bread onto a staff that they rode between

their legs. Crazy, but the drug was absorbed into their vaginas and it made them hallucinate and dream. That's why witches were always dancing naked in the forest; they were getting off on their own femininity without the need of men. These women played with herbs and were healers with a very strong high vibratory access, which pissed people off. Though if you messed with a witch, bad shit would happen to you and the witches were blamed.

Actually, the witches did not make the evil spells happen by themselves, they just tapped into the laws of cause and effect and karma was accelerated. As witches were misunderstood and burned at the stake, they left behind a vibrational field that was healing and not filled with remorse or rage. Maybe I am making this up, but as with Jesus, the holiness of highly vibrational beings will always rise up again and again against evil and darkness, even when they're no longer physically around.

As far as making things up goes, some of us just tap into alternate stories with elevating perspectives–that's how fairy tales came to be. Therefore, by tapping into elevated oscillations, it's true that we're doing hocus pocus, though the difference is that the Good Witch is invocating an "*Open Sesame*" aspect on the higher planes and is flying high on the broom while tapping into other realities. Imagery is the wand used while perusing the aisles of the higher planes. A dash of this, a pinch of that; we must swirl our visions together to create the new brilliance most needed.

Our imagination oscillates in infinite realities as visioning

happens on evolved frequencies. Therefore, always dream of the impossible, go mind shopping for your happiness, wish yourself well, wish everybody well (total mastery) and hang out in the wellness zone of harmonious cadences. Letting go of what has a low vibration elevates situations and brings us into the higher realms where our real sustenance is. So never be stuck in this one small reality, instead stay expansive, stay holy and grow your wings, even if they're ethereal.

Tapping into other realities, the broom is not a vehicle by itself, but symbolizes the sweeping aside of dirt: a ritual tool that whisks away negative astral energy to disinfect moods. A broom by the front door protects the house, a broom by the bed protects you while you sleep (a black onyx crystal works too). The witches were not only riding brooms, but also jumping across a broom on the floor to promote fertility. Jumping the broom is done in an African American wedding ceremony to bless the new couple in settling down together and to clear the way for their good future. I jumped the broom at a friend's wedding, and it was quite powerful.

Right now, we're lifting off of one frequency and moving into another. The aspect of the leap is our escalation into a higher state of being. Sometimes this happens quickly so we might lose our bearings and have to catch up to ourselves. As things suddenly shift, we don't know what's going on, things no longer work, everything appears to be on a delay because we've ricocheted into the next level of being and we have to acclimate. I always use my cat as a barometer; sometimes she dreams for days, then suddenly she's up, running around,

exploring new places to peruse the view from. It's like she's telling me not to look at things in the same old way when she's hanging out on the upstairs balcony railing, looking down at me in the living room.

Witches and cats have always been an item. An Egyptian myth suggested that cats were the embodiments of Gods and should be worshipped. Cats have been linked to the occult; they're known to have mysterious airs with intuitive skills and to chase away unwanted spirits. They guard the energy around loved ones and bring good fortune. A black cat crossing your path is good luck and whoever said otherwise was wrong, though if you believe it, take thirteen steps backwards and the bad luck will clear. Is it true? It's what you believe.

I've always had cats, and recently adopted a new one to keep my other cat company. My new cat has very strong love energy; she's friendly to all who come around but is very attached to me–she follows me everywhere. This cat is totally attuned to the vibrations happening around me and if I get upset, she becomes aggressive in a protective way. The first time I witnessed it I was shocked. I had accidentally stepped on my other cat's tail in the dark middle of the night on my way to the bathroom. When that cat hissed, I yelled, "Shit!"

My new cat came running out of the bedroom in attack mode: she was responding to my negative vibration. She does it every time I'm out of balance, so I have to be careful to keep myself in check, as no moods or negative vibes are allowed around her. This cat is a vibration guard who is

holding me to maintaining a high resonance. Feline beings are magical healers and heart openers who find us when we need their good energy. My cat is a teacher of mastery and the Universe sent her to me so I would stay in check. Some of us don't get a day pass on lower dimensional behavior; we can't afford to lose it or selfishly fall into an all-about-me mode.

The Good Witch knows about offerings; she knows that raising our vibration is the highest contribution we can offer. Since everything has a vibration, our energy field oscillates with the vibrations were in contact with. When I was in nasty bitch mode there was an enhanced bitch vibe around me, so others we're always trying to take me down with gossip, slander, vicious back-stabbing and so on. When the vibrations are low, we must change them and even though I've since shifted those lower vibrations, it took a while to clear the old energy field. This taught me that we still have to clean up the energetic mess we've made. We must clean it out on every level, from our victim consciousness, to feeling bad about past actions, to continuous thoughts that don't support a light-filled arena. Every emotional agitation we've held needs a scrub down, even after we've changed our minds. It's vibrationally cleansing to check ourselves into mental rehab, while the test is to hold our higher vibration strong even when its reverb hasn't clicked in yet.

At the same time that we're clearing the darkness out of our psyche, it's important to cleanse the bigger picture around ourselves. I meditate on clearing the energy I created in the

town I live in, and then I expand it to the city I come from and onto the entire east coast. I imagine a pink cloud of love expanding over these areas that is erasing any dark sludge I'd left behind. Imaginings are powerful reflections that shift dynamics and hold light where needed. It's mandatory to be aware of our unconscious behaviors, our judgments, our fears, and if we're contributing to the darkness or towards a light field. Our reactions are the barometer of where we are on the affecting scale, as things don't change until we change first. So, if someone's mood or frenetic energy is spewing craziness, my best reaction is to step aside so there is nothing for it to connect to. When I don't, I'm sucked in as all my energy is now involved and I'm left exhausted.

One of my shaman friends shared a protection healing she does daily for herself, with a visualization that she implants into her solar plexus. She visualizes a dandelion before it flowers, the kind you blow on to make a wish. She then visualizes blowing the seeds out of her being in a ten-foot radius around herself and instills the seeds with light. She sees herself standing in a mass of these scintillating, light-filled seeds and states that no dark energy may penetrate this auric field. She then pulls all the light seeds back into her solar plexus and it's done. Her invocation is sealed by her belief and it protects her. She surrounds herself with light and does not invest in dark energy, only light energy, which does its job on all levels.

This shaman clears dark energy that has been sent to people and once when she did a huge clearing on me, I

asked her what the bad energy was and who sent it. She said she didn't know as once she'd cleared it, it was totally gone, and she no longer had access to it. She taught me, when shifting up lower vibrations, never think about them again, just delete them. We are curious humans, always looking to see if the big it is still around and still, as powerful magical beings, when we decide it's not around—then it's not.

Every evening in bed, I visualize myself immersed in a beam of indigo blue light, it's my protection visualization that has an immediate hook-up with my higher self. I am joining up with my soul spirit to request their iridescence come into me. I then feel a white glitter energy and waves of bliss descend down upon me as a higher vibration covers me up for sleep. I do similar visualizations on my house, my car, my loved ones, stores, letters, and everything that needs to be uplifted. When I do this for other people, I always ask their higher self for permission first. There is one person in my life who, when I asked them in spirit to do this healing on them, I heard a definitive *No*! In reply, I instead send constant love their way and pray for them to receive healing from the source that is with them. We all have a divine source, be it ancestors, Angels, Gods or Saints. It's important to dialogue with them, as they're powerful healers who remind me they've got this, and we can take a moment to breathe and rest, so we can recharge.

Prayers for others, wishing them the best, seeing them in their highest light. is an offering that works. My prayers are now a co-creation with the God force I believe in. It used to

be me begging for a reprieve, as in "*Please make this happen.*" Now, my prayers are a decree that behest the co-guarantee I have with God. Like . . . "*God, I command that so-and-so find the way to their success now. Thank you! It is done, it is done, it is done!*" I no longer beg God to fix things but pass on my most sincere intentions to manifest with this supreme force as a co-creator. Sometimes the manifestations don't arrive in my exact package, instead they come as a test or a prelude to a transition, and it's with supreme faith that I still believe the blessings are a work in process.

If you ask your God source for a co-guarantee on a decree, you will get an answer. You will get direction and ideas will flow. If this is not happening, you are listening more to yourself than your source. If you are not receiving new concepts it's a message that you need to strip yourself down until you get to your ego and declare to this swagger of self-pride: "*With the force of my highest good, I am no longer following your direction!*" Once we do this, we have ordained a new decree and will be supported to come from our higher aspect.

We own old world magic; it's deep inside us, though for many it has been buried or smudged out by social and wrong-way consciousness. This magic is being sparked to surface now and will arrive first in imaginary ways. If you ask a child to come up with imagining a healing meditation, you'll get many wonderful variations of hocus-pocus, as it's our inner child who believes with all his or her heart in the

imaginary abracadabra. So, like shamans, we constantly have to retrieve this inner child to do the "*Open Sesame*" for us when we can't.

We didn't come here to grow up, we came to grow, and our inner child is an expert at growing things into action. It's all about the conversations we have with ourselves, as our experiences are reflections that mirror what's actually going on and where we need to uplift our conversations. And, since our inner child talks to invisible friends, he or she also talks to him/herself out loud while they're working something out. A child's world is our best relationship to ourselves; those conversations are golden even if they make no sense. So, if you've lost your mojo, hang out with children and let their vibration permeate your energy field. If suddenly you want ice cream or a lollipop, don't be surprised.

The pseudoscientist, Masaru Emoto, had proven that human consciousness affects the molecular structure of water, and it happens in the same ways that humans affect the vibrations around them. Since all relationships hold changeable frequencies, we're like a glass of water that's holding a vibration. Emoto saw that prayers could also clear polluted water, so our sacred visualizations mixed with heartfelt charisma do the same. It's amazing to understand the power of vibration and use it.

We all know people who are a drag to be around as their polluted unconsciousness is leaking into the atmosphere. Children and animals instantly react to these negative vibrations because they are full-on empaths. Empaths are

sensitive beings having the traits to pick up on the mental state of another presence. Mind you, we all have this vein of empathy, but some of us are like live wires that are on all the time—we pick up on everything and have highly tuned senses. It's kind of torture to be this sensitive, but on the other hand the intuitive gifts are great assets. As empaths, we have to find outlets to clear all the vibrations we pick up on. We also have to know when what we're feeling is not ours, as we're human vibrational vacuum cleaners.

Being an empath, I have a hard time going to restaurants and sometimes have to move tables many times. My son, when going out to dinner with me, waits outside the restaurant until I'm settled. He can't deal with my moving around, especially during the times I have to leave an establishment altogether. Recently, at a family dinner, I was fine at a table until a man sat down near us; he was having drinks and cursing excessively. His energy felt like a battering ram, and I said, "We have to move tables." My son refused. I at least got him to switch seats with me, so I would not be in the line of fire of this man's bad energy. After the dinner, my son said the man was saying despicable things to his tablemate and he too felt the bad energy. The difference is that my son can handle it, while it deeply affects me. If we were playing football, my son would be a good blocker, while I'd be the receiver running out to catch the drift.

As an empath, my intuition is always online; I see things that flash by, I read energy fields and receive messages in everything, though I constantly have to clear myself of other

people's energy. If I walk into a place of stressed-out people, my nervous system goes haywire until I ground it. Low vibrational energy clears when you hold a higher vibration to it, so when we say, "I'm not letting myself get upset," we're un-investing in the energy of another person, place, or thing, and empowering ourselves to move around it. If it's too late and we've slid into a dark lane, or been vampirized by some needy type, then we need to clear and come back into our highest essence. In public, when overwhelmed I have to find a quiet spot—a bench, the back of a taxi, even a bathroom—to neutralize my energy field. I imagine standing under waterfalls, on beaches, or pulling etheric CBD oil into my being to calm down. In point, I'm aware of what's going on around and inside me and constantly have to balance things.

There was a period when I felt allergic to my job and I couldn't do it, so I figured out all these ways to pass it off onto an assistant while I did other things. Dreaming of change, I walked beaches, traveled, read, wrote books, and lost myself in yoga. My anxiety was hanging out on level ten, always prodding me with dark imaginings. In the bigger picture, this was an important occasion, as I needed to take a reprieve and do it with a high vibration in order to shift. When I comprehended the necessity of my escape, it became the balm I calmed myself down with to continue on. I had no idea of the outcome but knew I was taking amnesty to visit my soul source for revitalization. After this excursion, I came to understand that I love real estate and always will—it's the hunt for creative aspects that thrive in habitats.

As things change, the energy of what's no longer magic is saying, *look for me not here but in other forms.* In looking around, I realized that what I'm looking for is not out there, and to look right at where I am with new perspective. As the polymorphic thrust continues to push us off our toadstools, we're not comfortable, nor should we be, especially if we don't agree. I'd felt stuck and I found it wasn't in a job or any one place–it was in a mindset. Feeling cemented in mundane realities, if we're not afraid, we get out of them by shifting our vision. I was too focused on the *what is*, and the *what if*, and as soon as questioned *what for*, I found meaning I could align with. Reasoning is valid as it explains why we need a certain outcome. I needed to feel virgin passion for the same old thing, which only became new again when I did.

During the COVID-19 quarantine, I felt comfortable stepping away from worldly things, as solitary time is a blessing to me. Moving into the fifth dimension, a higher form of reality based on using alchemy to disconnect from fear and move towards love, I ascended. Taking time to remove distortions, trauma, and sublimations from our psyche gets us unstuck from conditioning. Shocked, we may spend a moment trying to hold onto old ways, though when we can't let go of what no longer works, we're pulled back instead of pushed ahead. As lightworkers we're letting go and riding the wave into a new paradigm. Acknowledging that we came here for this exact moment in time, to be part of this magnanimous transformation, we have unlimited ethereal support. Meanwhile, the old reality is still running

beside the new one while it disassembles itself.

The Good Witch lives in her own high-vibrational world, yet still walks in the crazy world. At this point, I've learned to call on Good Witch to come and get me when I'm not her. I learned this from my niece, who, when she did bad things, would say, "That was not me!" It was true, who she really was, was a shining light of good energy—and when she wasn't, it was obvious she'd lost herself. It's important to track when we're not in our right lane and pull over to redirect ourselves. Things will lighten up as soon as we realize it's not us, though funny how we always ask, "Is it me?" At times, when having the courage to see the truth, it *is* us. When we pick up on vibrations, see behind masks, read the energy that's running, take apart behavior patterns, change lanes and don't look back—it's totally us!

Our bodies are receivers; the vibrations we hold are either healing or aggravating. I became furious at a situation and within moments I felt so pissed off that I became ill. I immediately went to a bench to calm down and shift my vibration. In minutes, I was fine. That's how fast both dynamics affect us, we either go down or up, so whatever's going on, we must choose to decline or affect any situation. An awake being is not swept away by vibrational waves but rides them. An enlightened being is one who is holding more light than not and creates waves from his or her light field. Since we are receivers, we must go to the universal field for inspiration and use our visualizations as our alchemy. Nikola Tesla described himself as electricity in human form and that his imagination gave birth to his experiments,

which were gifts to this planet. As Tesla said, "*If you want to find the secrets of the universe, think in terms of energy, frequency, and vibration.*"

Bad Bitch has raised her vibration and when she has to throw love bombs in the face of anger, she's doing it for herself to shift the energy because she now knows better. Real bitches always know better and the new version of Bad Bitch is still on target to take no shit, nor sling any, though she continues to bring up the shit in order to decimate it. As I look back on myself as a nasty bitch, I own her and it's a sorry/not sorry attitude I have about her, because she is a perfect teacher. I had to be her to survive and when I no longer needed to act out on her platform, we morphed. The important thing is to always be morphing, don't get lost in the low-down, just use it, peruse it, and find its springboard. It's not about being all airy-fairy; it's about truth. Sometimes truth is dark and not nice, it hurts before it heals, so we get in there, we roll up our sleeves, and we dig out of the crap even when covered in it. We don't have to be a better person—instead we raise the vibration around ourselves and the rest happens as it will.

Last, there's a big difference between really raising a vibration and twisting things around to look better. A friend who was in business bed with a selfish partner made non-stop excuses around why his partner was a good person. The egotistical partner took advantage of my friend for years, while my friend kept claiming this man helped him become successful. True, the man gave my friend his first big break in

business, but my friend didn't owe him for the next few decades.

One day the partner went too far: he'd preached the Buddha, boasted enlightenment and didn't pay a huge commission owed. It was a knock on the head when my friend saw the truth. Now in his sixties after thirty years of doing business with this fellow, he had to reinvent himself. Mind you, he still thinks his partner is a good man. Looking at a truth like that hurts, it's dark, it makes us question what in ourselves doesn't see the whole story. The point is that sometimes in the act of raising our vibration, we need to take off the rose-colored glasses and get damn upset. We don't just fix it, instead we let what's disturbing change us. Once that happens, we can no longer go back to who we were, and in this supreme shift, we raise our vibration—and follow it!

Elevating Our World

- We run on vibration so whatever's going on, use it to elevate off of. Everything has potential for us to uplift from, including anger, sadness, anxiety—all of it.
- Volatile emotions are a vibrational alert, telling us something needs to shift.
- Use your anger as a high sign telling you that you need to raise your vibration above it. Anger has value—it's fuel. Instead of spewing it, transform it to shift energy. We can use anger's power to do something affirmative, for instance: I was so angry I

reassessed my relationship and decided to no longer magnetize that dynamic in the future.

- In reassessing what we magnetize, we also change and hone in our reactions to veer higher.
- Someone is ranting to me on the phone, and I feel myself sinking. We can't talk the other out of it, but energy is viral. My get-off-the-phone line is: "*I have another call; I have to call you back.*" We're calling ourselves back from being involved.
- Whenever we're brought down, we need to do maintenance on our service plan. The service plan is our agreement to stay buoyant in the reality we want to thrive in.
- Someone has been lying to us, but we know their good side, so we keep letting them get away with it. Something's missing, it's our Self-Love, which has a very high vibration. We don't need years to heal our wounds—just by loving ourselves, we come into resonance with love and elevate out of wounds.
- When you feel overtaken by a low resonance, light a white candle in your mind and use it as a symbol of how to oscillate above it.
- In these turbulent times, consider yourself as an usher with a flashlight in the theatre helping others find their seat. The seat is the place where we rest with our soul and to be an usher, we must have a strong light.

- Move energy, pray, do mantras, sing, move your body, do yoga, exercise, cry, write, paint, play with children, love animals, always be smudging, and eat chocolate once in a while.
- Don't get lost on the Internet, don't check your phone every ten minutes, and turn the alerts off. Do read books for at least an hour a day, talk to people, walk in parks, meditate on benches, focus on plants and see if you can notice them breathe, get lost in wonder and look for magic in every possible way.
- Bless and send love to idiots; this includes one's own self when we've yelled out car windows, been rude to the waitress, and don't have compassion. It raises our vibration to own the fact that we can be assholes at times.
- Find irony, have humor–laughter is medicine.
- Instead of reacting, just acknowledge.
- Instead of backing away from low energy fields, elevate.
- Instead of arguing, enhance.
- We can move through crowds, leaving a trail of enlightened sparks.
- There's no need to constantly agree with the vibration that's running, we just need to live with what we're in agreement with–which might be the disagreement in itself.
- There's always a milestone in every incident; the power of progression happens even at the garbage

dump. When we find life's turning point, we've arrived at our next occasion. Don't get lost in circumstances, just find your blessings in them.

- Fear is one vibration and fearlessness is another. Fear tells us to use the now to transcend, while fearlessness is the horse we ride on.
- Give others the space to fix themselves by empowering them with the trust to do so.
- Trust your heart over your mind.
- In service to loved ones, we can ethereally untangle the webs they're caught in, so they can free themselves–it's called imagining the best for them.
- The benefit of a doubt demands that we prioritize what's most valuable, so look to what's outstanding and empower it.
- When it appears that a person has crossed you, don't get lost in judgment about it. It's more about our revelations around their actions than our emotions about it.
- It's a gift to see the truth in people, even when it hurts.
- Hanging out with the saint in our temple unveils a treasure.
- It's a blessing to see what was once invisible and be grateful for it.
- The highest vibrations are paved with blessings.
- Low vibrations are dysfunctional–shift them.

- Vibrations fluctuate and will adapt to the highest energy field in the area.
- The faster we drop what's not sacred, the quicker what is will appear.
- The more light we can hold, the more we affect vibrations.
- Invest in the vibration you wish to live in and surround yourself with it.
- The highest vibration is an energetic directive that guides us.
- A feeling that something's over means that there's no longer any juice to thrive on there.
- If you don't know where you're going, but the vibration is one of excitement, keep going.
- The preferred choice of which path to take is the path that holds the highest state.
- When we stand in our highest state, we liberate everything around us. When we live in our highest state, we liberate ourselves.

FEARLESSNESS
The Exorcism of Dread

"We've all arrived here fearlessly, we had to be fearless to get here.
We now have to live fearlessly–in order to really live."

The negatives we fear are only phantoms blaring loudly to be cured, as they're asking to be mended. What's going on is scary as Hell, and no doubt we've ended up in a compromised way where we can't count on the powers that be to take care of us. Nevertheless, to run through this crazy episode on fear separates us from our personal power—our inner super-hero. We all have this sleeping giant inside, and we have to wake them up, embrace them, and show up for ourselves as them. There is no alternative other than to be fearless in the face of demise, so go to that dark place where your disbelief in goodness exists and confront it from there. Listen to the stories fear tells, then step into your power and take them all down!

Wrong reasoning and fear are best friends, they back each other up, while audacity proves them both wrong. Audacity says: *"Fine, go ahead and fire me, leave me, bring on the worst, and I*

will find my way around it." The purpose of fear is to inspire fearlessness, and once we see this ulterior motive, we don't back away, instead we become brave allies with the bogeyman. In a conversation with fear about the end of my world, maybe the fifth one of the day, the Good Witch zooms in on the chat to let me know that I'm stepping into a magnanimous new world, while wise rational says: "*There's a reason for this–find it!*"

Bravery is on our agenda these days and it yanks us off the couch. How many hours have we spent in a frozen spasm while our mind is busy perusing the hysteria zone? When we know better, valor drops in and says: *Choose your reality, even if it seems impossible, choose it anyway!* I've learned never to go comparison shopping around other people's realities, to stay in my reality, to accept where I am and see what's good about it, even when it looks bleak. The bleakness is only a perception that my vision is off, and I need to blink it back into where the magic is. We're doing a visionary power-point right in the midst of our fearfulness and mind you, I wrote this book for myself as an affirmation of what needs to be going on–as the most courageous act is to not follow other people's bad ideas, and to stay loud in our hearts.

Scenarios with life-transforming aspects go to break us; they are really breaking us away from what we cling to. Mostly, we cling to wrong reasoning and a lack of acceptance for what is happening that feels outrageously wrong. Of course, we don't accept it, as when life becomes insane, it would be insane to agree. Though when we're on the roller coaster and can't step off, we have to surrender to the ride. I

find that when I'm liberated in my surrenders, I'm released from the fear. When we acknowledge that what's happened is done and we place our trust on the higher plane, I swear it's as if we're quickly lifted off our dark reality and are able to find a way around it.

I have a relationship with someone close to me that disrupts my wrong-lane side trips. This person will argue and demand that I stop and listen to his perspective, which might take hours to consummate. The reason? He is on an excursion and doesn't know where he's going until he gets there. He has to find what he's saying and thinking and demands my company. I gyrate on these rollercoaster trips, as once I'm on, I can't step off until we land. My ego gets mostly shattered, and I want to scream for help, so I quietly do, inside. I love this person dearly, and for the fact that he's a visionary genius, I show up. Where we usually end up is life-altering and changes the way I think and go. That's because where he goes is mind-bending, as he shakes up concepts and questions authenticity. A simple conversation with this person can address deep-seated fears and disseminate them, but that only happens after new concepts wrestle us to the ground in the art of release. This person is my son; he is not afraid to go to Hell with me and show me where I have not owned my Super-Hero-ness.

Imagine having a person in your life who demands that you step up to the plate on facing past and present traumas and dissipate them with self-love. Sometimes we have to do it because someone we love needs us to be the huge powerful version of ourselves to show them it's possible. Other times

we have to do a bravo move to show ourselves we're packing some ethereal big guns, and we might go down, but that's only because we're busy loading our guns. Who we are and how we carry our loads affects our loved ones; it affects the energy fields. The days of *show me your trauma and I'll show you mine, and we will be best friends over our shared traumas,* are over. It's now about show me your courage to move on and heal, so I can follow your lead.

It's a wake-up call when we recognize that we've invested a major part of our life force in following directions that are not sustainable. It's another wake-up call when we realize we wrote the directions and agreed to them. Then again, all paths will lead an awakened mind to freedom once we begin to think on this wavelength. Awareness is the path to fearlessness that turns on our inner lights to expose the shadows. This is not easy, as the resistance alone is like a dark basement with no windows, so we don't want to go there. Yet if we don't confront our dark side, our fears and our angst, then those things own us.

Terrifying realities want to control us; they are really just alerting us to our weaknesses around things going out of control. Our fears tell us that we too have lost our control, when in truth it's that we have lost our courage to cowardice. There is serious danger in aligning with angst in that it has direct access to our motherboards, which creates the perfect alignment of circumstances for us to be brainwashed by. Here, we're taken advantage of, lied to, and manipulated, and once we react, fear has us in its clutches and suddenly we're lost in it. In the same way that we have prescriptions

for optical weakness, medicine for illness, and food for thought, when we shine a light on fear, it will lose its power and no longer be able to knock our lights out.

A friend moved into a newly constructed exclusive residence in Manhattan. On her first evening in this new apartment, she crossed paths with a rat in her living room. In a delicate state, she screamed hysterically, completely losing it. Immediately upon her calling me, the rat ran into one of the bedrooms while my friend was off the rails, totally imagining that her new home and building was infested with rats. The super came up and found the hole in the wall where the rat had entered and told her this was a rare situation resulting from the recent construction in the entire building and that this had never happened before. Within minutes my friend texted me that she was going into that bedroom commando style to retrieve something she needed in there. What she was really retrieving was the power she lost that would support her fearlessness. Once we do this, it doesn't mean that shit won't happen—it means that we won't fall apart when it does.

Copious dark energy fields sometimes surround this Good Witch; she laughs and waves her wand at them, telling them to lighten up. Bad Bitch has spent hours in bed with her demons, listening to unhelpful voices, while her nervous system had viral flares of *What if, what if, what if?* Immersed in her fear and no longer in the moment, she'd abandoned her present existence and is traveling into a nebulous future that hasn't yet materialized, and she's fueling it. It's called

paranoia, being a fear-based certainty that possesses us to behave reactively by ethereally solidifying our fears. We must pull our energy out of these black holes, step over the cracks, and change the channel on fear-based thinking.

The Good Witch knows that the darkest demons are the flying monkeys in our own minds, and all the black candles and spells in the world won't touch them. We can smudge and clean our auras till the cows come home, but those effin flying monkeys won't quit till we serve them some chamomile tea or CBD oil and have a nice chat with them, while taking our power back. What do I do when my fears start whispering in my ear about how, when I'm old (which might be now) I will be desolately sitting on a sidewalk with my cat, begging for money? I remind them that if they don't shut up, *they* will be on the sidewalk because their stories are bullshit. I am constantly talking to my fears, as in, "*You're allowed to warn me of realistic cautions, like don't walk down that street, or don't trust this person, or go get the car serviced, but you're not allowed to affect my future.*"

A friend in my town battled ovarian cancer for six years and she would always state to the cancer, "You will not own me or run my life!" She had a beaming smile and was a true warrior who cherished every day, even the bad ones, as she had supreme gratitude for simple things. When hard times grab me, I think of her and how she would focus on love and the things that brought her bliss, and my thoughts of her would shift me. She died on Easter Sunday, in the middle of the Coronavirus Pandemic. So many people in my town

showed up, masked, distanced but brought together by her great spirit. If anything, she touched several of us, giving us a message: Never give up, always be in love, and don't let darkness win. That's the wave she rode out on and she left its reverberations for others to live on, as her legacy.

Circumstances come up and what's going to happen may happen whether we worry about it or not. Someone we love might die, we might lose our home in a fire, there could be a car accident, or we might send our children to school with our hearts in our hands worrying about a possible gunman or the virus. Nevertheless: we still get on the plane, we go to the supermarket during a pandemic, we send our children to school with cell phones that work, we will try to get loved ones in recovery when necessary, and we always do our best. This means we won't stop living, hoping, and believing in goodness. If something happens that breaks our heart, then we will live broken-hearted and we will have the opportunity to grow and heal from our grief because in the end, all the love we've ever had is ours forever. The loss of our loved ones shows us the connection is always strong across all dimensions. It means it's time to bridge into our hearts that beat into eternity—and that's how we stay connected to love.

An antidote to fear is to love what exists now and feel worthy of good fortune, no matter what's happening. Worrying will not help, but communication with the power person we are, and being in communion with our Divine Spirit will. So, talk to yourself from the higher perspective, speak to others and address fear directly, find the channels

to come to peace around what is. From here, see what you can use in the situation to elevate from while taking time for your healing. A date with a conscious commitment to healing brings us to what we honor over doubt. When the Good Witch is slapped, she turns the other cheek towards herself to see where her cure-all is and considers the slap a wake-up call.

My wake-up call came in the realization that if fear was an abandoned crying child in need, the conversation we would have with them, the care and love we would offer that would calm them down is what's needed in our self-dialogues. "*So, hello fear, you think that I will be on the sidewalk, that I'm a failure, that a catastrophe is on its way. Well, here is my reality: If I'm on the sidewalk, it's because I'm hailing a cab; if I'm a failure, I will learn from it and try again. If a catastrophe comes, I will call out my inner hero and do my best to survive while helping others. Meanwhile, fear, you can continue to state your concerns that are mostly about the future, and I will continue to remind you that here in the now, even when darkness is looming, the ecology is in crisis, politics are scary, loved ones are grieving, and I might be grieving–faith is holding me though all of it. Because I've blessed myself to live in love and will continue doing what needs to be done!*"

On a day when an old friend threw me to the curb over a real estate deal we were working on together, she was on the edge and not in her right mind. I held strong to my belief that her craziness was none of my business. Fear had made her greedy, while her ego acted like a gorilla thumping its chest; it was a power struggle. The question was, should I

walk away from a job that I'd worked on for a year? Colleagues all felt I should hang in there and not walk away. Fear said, "*Oh, here you are, screwed again, this is your bad karma, now you will suffer.*" Realizing that my real sustenance comes from the Universe and not from a business deal, I spent the day aligning with the highest vibrations I could muster and asked my Divine Spirit for assistance in not hooking into bad feelings. Within hours, I felt empowered to carry on.

Granted, this was serious work. I'd rolled up my sleeves and done battle (mostly with myself), coming to terms beyond fear and sadness to reach a resolution: I might lose money on this deal, but I still owned my power. This broker friend had said three things to me that struck me and sealed my truth. The first thing said was, "You always have to win." True, in real estate I play to win for everyone involved. The second was, "You are always on your high horse." Only true when I am on my way to a closing and feeling great about my success. The third was, "You used to be a better broker." Totally false: I am the same genius broker I always was, only now I'm particular in what I choose to work on because I can be.

It's a joke to try to control the way other people act as I deter myself from working with people who cheat, have no ethics, and lack consideration. Sometimes fate will throw me into the pot with this dynamic, just so I can learn mastery. Meanwhile, my fears are in constant protest over this personal growth, as in: *You're crazy, just go for the money or you*

will be broke. In retaliation, I tell fear that I have an enhanced quality of life and will always get by. At the end of the day, this broker friend calmed down and apologized. Fine, I'm a forgiver.

I hung in on the listing, but now the sellers were threatening that we would be fired if we did not sell their house in three weeks. My broker friend was then the one who wanted to quit, but I refused. Since I play to win, I upped the ante and buried a St. Joseph statue at the property (Saint Joseph is the patron saint of home sellers). I then had a conversation with the Universe, did my Abracadabra, and surrendered the endeavor to all possibilities. A week later, I ended up selling the house myself. Mastery over emotions will always pay off, as it's the ability to feel fear and not empower it. The Good Witch was whispering her innuendos into my psyche, though it was my Badass Bitch who hung in there saying, "I'm not quitting!" The difference was that Badass Bitch didn't tell anyone off but kept a one-pointed focus on what was needed and went there. Mastery is a rebel auditor that goes to the power place and demands that it perform.

My Badass Bitch is fearlessly aligned with her Good Witch accomplice and together they're like a walking flashlight that uncovers shadows and displaces angst. Mostly, we go to the mirror to shine light on ourselves—we're like glow-worms that shine in the dark when we're on. The trick is to turn ourselves on, so we flip the switch, swat away the do-da, and face ourselves. What we're facing is our audacity

to shine no matter what. Even knowing when to let go, when to surrender, and when to change is rugged power. Granted, it's an intense time and we're delicate, but the fact that we've all traveled through a birth canal and survived makes us innately durable and strong. We were made for this ride because we all have the tenacious vein somewhere inside us and it's time to tap into it.

During the time when I felt allergic to my real estate business, fear thought it was my new best friend and was always hanging around. At the same time, my husband was dealing with chronic Lyme disease, which feels like spirochetes of fear warriors roaming around in one's body. It was a very difficult time that affected both of us, causing us many periods of emotional paralysis. I wondered how the Hell we could move forward if we were both dysfunctional, and this is where grace came in. If you could imagine a hero arriving on a white horse; I was in constant prayer when suddenly grace showed up to reveal a healing process that would restore my husband to health. It was a protocol that would take a while, maybe two years, but it would work. In six months, there was light at the end of the tunnel. Beyond fear, anger and feeling frozen, the situation demanded priorities, so everything that was not important went to the back burner; it was a defining time of focusing only on our quality of life. The challenge was to get on that white horse and ride through it all. We did.

Badass Bitch is a risk-taker, while Good Witch holds common sense for right action as a risk worth taking. As

confrontations arrive, it's a chance to purge what's in question. To question is to highlight what's integral to our quality of life. We don't take the easy road or the shortcut, instead we take the high road and while our fears are shrieking, we question their purpose to see where they'll take us if we allow them to pilot our lifestyles. These challenging intervals are showing us that it's now time to become our own warriors, heroes, and heroines. We must step forward with discipline and honor, armed not in defense, but with pure intentions. It was intent that pulled the sword from the stone; that sword is our power and the stone is our fear, so grasp your sword, pull it out of fear and own your faith. When you grasp your power, the stone will let go because fear has no real hold.

The Exorcism of Fear

- It's time to break all contracts on the subliminal agreements we've made with ourselves to become a certain way, especially when these contracts are based on protecting others or ourselves from certain weaknesses that we presume exist.
- Interrupt all patterns of long-learned, unconscious behaviors, like threats of withdrawn love and guilt trips, which only exist when we let them.
- Don't give any juice to dark force fields—practice moving right through them.
- Keep rising above all that is not your true way.

- Know that when hard times arrive and bring us to our knees, they will also empower us to get up again and walk in new ways.
- Use your pain as an accomplice and grow through it.
- When we sit in discomfort as a radical act to disperse it—it gives way.
- During the dark nights of our souls we're not alone, but in partnership with our Divine Spirits—take them by the hand.
- Don't engage in ego battles; clear away war-mongering relationships because they don't take us to paradise—only Love takes us to paradise.
- Stop wearing a suit of armor, take down the barriers, open your heart and know that your own right action is all the protection you need.
- Neutralize hostilities, don't take revenge, let the universe handle it.
- Love yourself more than you hate your disappointments.
- Don't let fear boss you around, do what you love anyway.
- Never align with angst—always align with faith.
- Nothing can control you when you're in control of your mind.
- Hear no evil, speak no evil, see no evil—don't listen to it, verbalize it, or look for it. No whining, complaining, or describing, leaves nothing for fear to attach onto.

- Put salve on your wounds and all that they did to you.
- Honor your inner hero.
- To not be ruled by fear, commit to a route beyond a mundane existence.
- Our hearts are fearless—they never lie, so when confused ask them for the truth.
- One who is on a heart mission is too ecstatically on a roll to be thwarted by fears.
- Acknowledge the fear, thank it for its warnings, and do what your heart decides.
- When we make fear less huge than it is, we become bigger than it.
- Our greatest fears hold the seeds to our liberation.
- What's happening out there has already been set in motion; what's happening inside us has not. To own and follow our empowered feelings—we put change into motion.
- Fear is an entity that needs to be heard, calmed down, and brought into balance.
- In our wholeness, there's only room for wisdom—fears push us to find our wisdom.
- Fear instills fearlessness when we sit with it, breathe into it and work through it.
- Our thoughts all have imaginative force—choose the ones with the highest resonance.
- Promise your fear that things will be okay, which gives it something to chew on besides your future.

This is all fear really wants to hear, because it doesn't understand the power of now.

- Consider what fear is doing to push you past it.
- Fear doesn't want to own us—it wants us to own ourselves.
- Therefore, do consider fear an ally; see anxiety as an exercise in mental strength, and depression as a message to press on—this is all part of the game of life.

CUTTING CORDS
Severing Bad Bonds

"With detachment we empower our freedom–with conviction we empower detachment."

The Good Witch knows there are spells involved in cutting cords on bad relationships with people who have done us wrong. What we're cutting cords on is the energy field around these happenings. If we don't cut the cords on these kinds of involvements and just cut cords on people, the same experiences will continue with new people. We need to go to the source beyond people by getting down to the storylines where these dynamics have been allowed. We need to change the stories that don't carry us, to new stories that do.

A friend who was in love with his wife went through a hideous divorce with her. She basically took him for everything he had, and then in order to make herself look less bad, she went around talking shit about how nuts he was. He called me in tears, saying all he ever wanted was to love her and have it be returned. It was good that he'd done his best towards her and we decided that while she was

spewing meanness, he would just keep sending her love. What he was doing was cutting the cords on being bitter and taking revenge by opening a door for a reciprocated love to arrive because he was still revolving in love. This higher way of being warrants doing the opposite of reactiveness when we're in despair.

Back to my friend who was trying to cheat me on the real estate deal; she was not a bad person per se, but rather an example of a dynamic that runs prevalent in my business. I decided not to hook into her bad behavior but instead to cut cords on those actions. This is not to mean that some realtors in my business would stop being greedy lying cheats. It means that I'm no longer going to be affected by them, and by this, I attract otherwise. In the end, my friend came around and did the right thing. Will she try to do the wrong thing again? Probably, but she'll never have the chance to do it again, because I'll never again be involved in a partnership with her.

In the practice of cutting cords, we visualize a rope that connects the core of a person or experience to us and then we envision severing the cord with a knife. We then visualize burning the ends of the cord and sealing both ends with wax. The purpose of this ritual breaks the connection. This doesn't mean we won't dial it back in mentally, it means we have done a ceremony around changing a relationship we don't want to continue with. The ceremony is our statement to the Universe that we are serious.

You can also place a disturbing dynamic in a bubble and

cut the cord on the entire bubble, sending it into a healing vortex. Instead of wasting time trying to fix unacceptable things, it's liberating to fling them out of our realms. In the case of family or karmic situations that we learn and grow through, to cut the cords on the emotional hysteria frees us to avoid throwing the baby out with the bathwater. We keep the love, dump the rest, and take ourselves higher in the situation. Mastery is our ability to acknowledge what's happening and maneuver through it or move it out.

On a day of intense energy rolling in like waves, I realized that I needed to cut the cords on my emotion centers that were bothered by an old relationship with a childhood best friend. This friend and I grew up in the same building; she came from a very wealthy family and always flaunted having more money than me. My family was wealthy too, but they were so dysfunctional it was at times embarrassing. This girl was always sending me shaming implants; the ones with *I-Am-Better-Than-You* put-downs. We might think we're imagining these back-biting things, though when we receive consistent messages with bad vibes around someone, we're not imagining it. Now, decades later, this old friend would show up always at the last minute, still extremely rich, looking for Hamptons August rentals.

I had uncomfortable feelings around her, while she still arrogantly flaunted her haughty wealth in my face. She'd call last-minute saying she needed at least ten thousand square feet in a *you-should-already-know-this* tone. The moment I heard her voice, my ill-fitting feelings around her surfaced, so I

planned to use this latest rental experience to release them. Instead, I released her forever. Well, the Universe did it for me. She'd had a fit when I did not have enough rentals to show her within the hour, and after I made an appointment for her to see one, she then told me she would rather see it with the listing broker. "As you wish," was my response. Relief came, and I decided I would no longer take her calls.

Moments later, the rental listing broker called me to say that she'd called him and told him she'd known me her entire life and owed me nothing. He said, "Then your friend won't get paid for the work she has done for you." And my old friend said, "That's okay, it's only a rental." The broker told me if she rented the house, he would personally pay me. The Universe was proving to me that there are still many good people around.

We may need to cut cords many times when we feel a charge around an experience, as the charge holds the lesson. I cut the cords on betrayals, on the conspiracy of evil, on hopelessness, on shame, on feelings of revenge, and on fear. We can also cut the cords on continued karmas that have played out from past lives. Think about it . . . you broke a lover's heart a few lives back and ever since you have been living these current lives with a constantly broken heart. When we do a healing on the past and ask for forgiveness, the soul memories and karmic cords are resolved. We can apologize anytime for anything we have done that was not of the highest accord, and that's something we do in spirit on a soul level. Maybe it's an event that seemed flippant and

didn't even affect the other party but energetically affects us, so it still needs to be addressed.

Sit and ponder on things that have happened in the past, including possible past lives, since we've traveled with loved ones over and over. When situations with others feel like old shit, it could be very old, like lifetimes old. This is an example of the things we don't address and clear that will come back around through eternity to be dealt with. Even if it's something you're imagining has happened—use it and make peace with it.

I have another friend whom I love and coincidingly feel great discomfort around. She has a *know-it-all* attitude and always offers unasked-for advice when you just want to have a conversation. Even though she's quite evolved, I distance myself for weeks when she irks me. I've experimented with cutting the cords on what bothers me about her and keeping the love. Once we identify our rooted feelings, we can trace them back to the core of an old occurrence and why it bothers us. For instance, if an experience brings up anxiety, a defense mode, or shame, we need to go deeper into our foundation and follow its footprint to where the original injury happened and change it from there. When I went to the root of my discomfort, I realized that about a decade ago I made a wrong decision. My ability to rationalize choices back then had gotten misconstrued. I then cut the cords to all the judgments I'd made about myself regarding my previous bad choice. As such, all the prior annoyances I had towards my opinionated friend quickly faded and I could laugh at her presumptions.

In reality, when cutting cords, maybe it's not the actual situation that changes, but our tolerance to it. The outside world doesn't just snap into transition for us; we change first and then it matches our advance—that's how we make headway. Our displaced feelings are gifts, as they point out the circumference of our motivations, where our energy leaks are, and what's toxic. To use our discomfort to decipher our hidden agendas clears the energy field in these stories that we carry, especially the ones that are blaming and catalysts for growth. My friend with the *know-it-all* attitude motivated me to check in on where I also think I know it all.

At a time when I was between the here and there on my future it wasn't helpful for me to be influenced or sidetracked by anyone else's opinions. This was a time to cut cords on the dynamic of running my discomfort by others to feel better. Especially with people who valued their own point of view over empowering others to find their way. I cut the cords on where it was in myself that was giving my power away to someone else's conclusion, in the sense that it felt wrong. Taking the time to know my own answers directed me to know when to ask for opinions and how to use them my way.

Sometimes what we think is going on is not even close to what's really going on and this just means we have to snap out of a *know-it-all* attitude. The dynamic running with the people closest to us shows us where we have to dive deeper. Interesting how when you get to the source of an issue, it shifts, as there's a point of departure on everything that

supported it. Therefore, we must clean up our stories, our bad beliefs, our wounds and traumas. It's amazing how, when we're in clean-up mode, the weirdest stuff from the past arrives for swiping. For example, while in the mode of clearing regrets, suddenly ones we didn't even know we had come into the limelight.

An old story I'm not proud of is when I was a young hair and makeup artist to many famous people, I was sent to the hotel room of Freddie Mercury, to cut his hair. At the time, I was not into the music of Queen and did not get who he was. Freddie had that haircut with the short bangs and needed it freshened up for his show that night. He was so kind to me, asking me my opinion on many things, about which I was not being helpful. I told him he should cut that hairstyle off. I was basically rude to him, leaving as fast as I could and never thinking about it again, until recently. A friend asked me to go see the movie *Bohemian Rhapsody,* which is about Freddie, as her daughter who had passed on loved him and Queen.

Sitting in the theatre and seeing the story of Freddie's life and how he really was his own hero, hit me so hard that I knew I was having a karmic repercussion on my bad behavior. I saw what a hard time he'd had, and in fact remembered he was a bit drunk and weepy when I met him. I felt so bad. I also saw how he was a musical genius and how stupid I was for being so closed off back then. I sat in the dark theatre and apologized to Freddie from the bottom of my heart. I sat and let myself feel ashamed and deeply sorry

until lightness surrounded me, and it felt as if I'd connected to the essence of Freddie and was forgiven. I then forgave myself. It might not seem like a big deal, the unconscious things we did when we were young, but our unconsciousness has veins that solidify storylines that don't serve us. So, every time we know we've done wrong, we do well to address it and clean it up, because we are always sweeping the path to our future.

Here's how to cut cords: Sit in a quiet space and ask to be guided to experiences where you or others have not acted well. Request that all attachments and dynamics that no longer serve your evolvement in these instances now be released and not be allowed to reattach. Then delve into your body and notice where you feel a reaction to these past experiences. For me, it's felt either in my heart, as in heartbreak, or as a knot in my stomach. Notice the areas affected and cut the cords from there. Then place your hands over these areas and do a self-healing by sending in love.

As far as heartbreak goes, grief needs to be felt deeply all the way to its delivery of grace. We're shifting what has influenced us toward what we want to ascend with, which is mostly love. Often when we clear ourselves, we don't know what new magnetism is arriving and must leave space for it. Consequently, after cutting cords we might end up sitting around with nothing going on. Consider this a space of pure magic where what's unfamiliar is being construed.

Funny, I was having a conversation with a wizard friend, who was telling me his plans for the future, which revolved

around shifting the influence of worrying about money. Mind you, I know people with tons of money who still have a present not-enough-money program running, so it has nothing to do with what we have. I mentioned to my friend that at times I, too, have this feeling and he said, "Anyone who has this feeling should immediately quit his or her job!" He was saying we should do the opposite of what we think is the natural order of trying harder and money-making. His premise is that if we're not in the flow of our charismatic energy a.k.a passion, because circumstances have changed–then we need to change.

A client, who was also a long-time past friend, told me he loved me again, after I made him a windfall of money on a real estate deal. I asked him if he didn't love me before? He said not as much. My Bad Bitch replied, "You don't love me, you love money!" Good Witch laughed and thought, some truths don't need to be held back. The client could not respond and in that moment, I realized I too love money, or I would not even be talking to him. I laughed along with my Good Witch, and then decided I was basically done with him. He reminded and empowered me to spend more time on my passion and to not always be going for the money.

It's a huge message that we're supporting our creative passion when we redirect our magnetic pull around abundance. My wizard friend asked me what I love doing the most, which is writing; it's something I'm always doing in tandem with selling real estate. I had changed the way I was doing my real estate business in the sense that I'd narrowed

it down to a quality of life I could resonate with while still doing it. Though what my friend was saying was more radical, like quit your job!

It's huge grist for the thinking mill to cut cords on anything that doesn't hold passion for us. Imagine that when you hate what you do for a living, you make a plan, and you cut down your overhead and then just quit. If that feels like an adventure that wakes you up, it might be something to consider. Then again, if you invest more energy in your passion, it leads to your abundance around it and puts you on a new path. It certainly takes balls, and ethereal balls work just as well when we can't find our actual human balls.

While I was at times battered by selling real estate, I felt a hatred for it. Thinking about it in a cord-cutting ceremony, I realized that humans are mostly battered by their reactions. I thought about the many things that bother me, from self-serving politics, to business values, to the rules of being successful, to not having control over things. I thought about false advertising and the fact that social media is a robber of my time that bleeds into almost everything. As I had my scissors out and began cutting, it occurred to me that being the hairstylist I was, if I kept cutting, I'd be bald. I stopped cutting and thought about what I loved, and by pulling these things forward they'd atomically override what I so disliked. Ding! It came to me that love cuts away the discomfort. I do love selling real estate. I love the hunt, the vision, negotiating the deal, and the closing. Therefore, if I'm occasionally battered, I will not let those aspects win. Instead, I decided

to trim around what I loved to make it more obvious. I was styling my passion, instead of cutting it off.

In quarantine, when only essential businesses were allowed, we had to change the ways we think about what we do for a living. We had time to delve into expansive concepts that pushed us to explore other options. We went virtual, we zoomed, we zoned out, zoned in, and held space for inspiration. We saw what was now needed and we figured out where we fit in to fulfill the new order of these times. In moments of grief, thinking about what I can offer: I am a fearless battered woman who is bleeding love. I find my balance in deep bliss and see the magic in the moonlight in ways I never have. The quiet, the non-excuses, the alone time, all becomes a gift where we face ourselves and find rectitude. We might be sitting in the nothing zone, waiting on standby, and holding a space open for our new creative walking orders. This is a time when we can no longer live the old ways as we're becoming part of the new. This occasion bears gifts and our rituals are to find them.

Another ritual while cutting cords on old versions of what doesn't work is to cut cords on anxiety, as it's not a family member and has no residence rights. Anxiety loves to visit in the in-between times and scratch its nails across the mental chalkboards we're creating our dreams on. I sit with anxiety and chant mantras to her and question where I'd be without her, while I roll up my sleeves and ground myself in freedom from this unease. Though first, I have a conversation with her prior to an eviction, it's a chat on why I let this angst in.

Anxiety is a liar that stops our dreaming and escorts us into a nebulous future that doesn't even exist. It has ruined relationships, distorted reality and cut off our flow of abundance. Going into the bigger picture lessens anxiety, while looking to past experiences of success, disowns it. I play with putting it into a bag of hot air where it belongs and mentally lighting it on fire. I've been doing battle with anxiety for years and have come to realize that she's a great teacher, pushing me out of constrictions, judgments, and hysterical feelings.

The conversation with anxiety is: How do you want to empower me as opposed to taking me down? Since anxiety is another bitch in my house, I demand answers. I heard within, she's here to talk me out of empowering her—and to instead empower myself. It might be a life-long battle that I have with her, just like the one I had with my mother. While *it is what it is*, the fact is that this dynamic is pushing us to find what it isn't. It isn't real! Though it's really annoying and needs to be moving out.

A tenant in a rental that I had to show for sale was undermining; he made the house look awful on purpose. The owners wanted the house shown, though this tenant tried to scare me with threats. I was worried. Anxiety had arrived and was messing with me; it made me feel like I was doing something wrong. I then realized this guy had nothing that could affect me, and I must go around him to continue to do my job. It was a question of who do we show up for? I was showing up for myself. I sold the house in spite of him

and he had to move out. I then addressed the momentary lack of faith I had in myself and moved that out too.

Last, never own the things you don't want. By talking about our anxiety, we're owning anxiety. The magic of the word Abracadabra means: "*Create as You Speak.*" Therefore, our words are wands, which create for us as we go. My pain, my grief, my broken heart, my patterns, my past, my shame, my fear . . . these are all fleeting states that we needn't own. Instead, we can use them to excavate our hero-ship. To declare our hero-ship, as in: *It was hard and I got through it,* is an Abracadabra statement. We all have the hero archetype in our mix; it's time to warrant this daredevil to empower us to come out as we truly need to be to get through hard times.

Power is not about thinking we have control, we don't, it's more about being in the now and dealing with it. My inner control freak loves to say things like, "Never again, I'm not going there, I will not be spoken to that way, I'm done." Who knows where we're actually going and what reality we can control? Really, we're here to show up for the labyrinth of discovery and adventure while cutting cords on the rest. Our hero is the wise one inside who doesn't back away but stands in the moment and finds the power place in it. Bad Bitch has found her power place in patience, in waiting out the Hellishness, and in trusting the bigger picture. "Patience is power," my husband always says. Trusting the Universe and believing that the world is not out to get me is what I sanction. Embracing my faith, I'm embracing the acceptance of finding my power place through whatever is happening.

On the way to the airport, while stuck in traffic, we might encounter anxiety and sitting there saying, "The traffic now clears" may not work, because maybe we're supposed to miss the plane. Maybe don't own the maybes either, just be in the moment. Get to feeling right about it, even if what feels wrong is flashing. Being in the moment of what feels right is an excavation process that shows us what cords we need to cut to get to our empowerment. So, when things feel like crap, start cutting the cords around it, and in this act alone we are coming into our power.

Early one morning, on our way to JFK airport, in the dark, we took a wrong turn and ended up in the deserted old World's Fair Park in Queens. We were driving around in circles, there were no exit signs, and in that moment, I decided it was fine if we missed the plane. In the next moment, a strange voice yelled through me to my husband, "Turn left!" He jerked the car left onto a side road, and immediately we were back on the expressway going to the airport. When I cut the cord on the expectations of having my trip go a certain way, and even accepted giving up the trip, a voice came through and we found our way. That's all we're doing here, finding our way. So, in the times we find ourselves in the jungle and the way is concealed, we must get out our machete and excavate a new one.

Evidence of Cords That Need to Be Severed . . .

- You find you are repeating the same scenarios over and over.
- You keep forgiving people who have wronged you and nothing changes.
- You focus on your dreams constantly, but they never come to be, as if they're blocked.
- There's always a lack of funds and you make excuses for why, mostly blaming the state of the world and your high values, which don't mesh with lowly world values.
- You hate your quality of life and don't do anything about it.
- Feeling hopeless, you no longer try to change things.
- You are so tired that you want to give up.
- You are constantly in the kinds of relationships that don't serve you.
- You keep calling up the same old memories, feeling that there's something you need to address there, but can't figure it out.
- You're holding onto things you can't let go of.
- You desire revenge.
- You need to be right.
- You always have to know what's going on.
- Believing your opinions matter most, you're not open to a mutual understanding.
- You're depressed and have no mojo.
- You feel there's something seriously wrong with you.

- You believe you're affected by evil and think someone has put a spell on you.
- You're blocked by your own negativity and keep wondering why things don't change.
- You blame others for your problems.
- You're self-righteous.
- You feel obsessed about someone.
- Your role models act insane and you think that's cool.
- You believe that the judgments and criticisms that others have toward you are either lies or completely true, and you no longer know who you are.
- You can't make decisions and your intuitive skills are shut down.
- Everything always goes wrong.
- You mentally argue with yourself, thinking about what you should have said or done.
- You can't think for yourself and have to run everything by someone else—your pendulum, your tarot cards, or your psychic.
- You don't learn from your mistakes.
- You're always on the defensive, on guard, expecting the worst.
- Escape into substances is your only relief.
- You use food for comfort and either starve or overfeed your body.
- You feel constantly sick and believe you will never heal.

- You are mostly never okay.
- You fake happiness.
- You live more in your social media presence than in real life.
- You have trouble sleeping.
- You want to isolate more often than not.
- You have no faith.

The entire evidence above means that our energy is not properly aligned. Even if we've been abused, it's time for us to completely heal. We start by addressing the issues, as by seeing what binds us to these controversies, we will know what to execute to become finished with them. Addressing emotions with the intention to heal them, as opposed to being lost in them, removes the first layer of symptoms; the second layer is reasoning. While we unravel, look for the patterns around the issues and focus on the cords around these issues that need to be untangled. We have to get the knots out, the places where we're bound in order to see where to sever those cords in order to heal.

The reasoning needs to be addressed, like when we're so tired, yet we can't sleep because there's an imbalance. We must focus on what the imbalance is saying and question what it needs. Maybe it needs us to get off social media hours before retiring and not drink too many coffees during the day, or it needs us to stop worrying about what we can't control and meditate before retiring. Our insomnia will tell us what it needs if we ask. So will a trauma, it will tell us that

we have to feel it to the core and then it will show us our heroine edge. If we trust our inner hero, we conquer the trauma.

Awareness demands that we identify and observe what needs to be severed before we cut, otherwise we're just slicing wildly, and nothing gets divided. In the cases where we keep repeating the same scenarios, get out the magnifying glass and stare into what you don't want to see. We're inspecting the story behind the story, the hidden stories. A key to the mystery is that every rotten story comes down to us doing the nasty to ourselves. When we untangle from what has wrangled us in, we become less paralyzed by these battles. We can then start the conversations we must have in order to liberate ourselves and once we recognize where we got captured, all the holds will dissolve. If they don't, then we must go deeper and look harder—we're excavating here!

How about the condition where you can't think for yourself and have to run everything by someone else, or your pendulum, or the like? Cutting the cords on neediness is required here, though first we need to address the dynamic where this was originally created and question what supported it and why. As we cut cords on these deeper aspects, we come to focus on the people who supported our neediness; possibly the guru types who need us to need them, or our mothers who need to be heard, or the parts of us that don't want to face truths, or maybe it's our denial that takes over in self-protection. Defining the issues and untangling them from our core beliefs is how we heal. The

objective is to delve into and sever those connections until we begin to feel empowered and come back to believing in ourselves. It will happen if these are our intentions and we're running toward their outcomes.

Imagine that sometimes we even have to cut the cord linking our own mind to our heart. Like when we're poisoning ourselves with toxic thinking, the solution is to notice everything going on within and undo what does not resonate. Once you begin doing this, big shifts happen, and your life force will come back. Meanwhile, many attachments fall away, unnecessary people go their way and helpful new people arrive. As we delve into this uplifted state, depression abates, we have room to breathe and extra space to dream. Once we've reconciled with ourselves, we become more and more powerful, our stance is solid, we don't need to overly question because we're intuitively connected, we're fearless, and up for an undertaking.

Ultimately, like Alice in Wonderland, this journey is an adventure. We've all landed in the rabbit hole, so naturally we might grow big or small a few times; but how we go is only between us and who we are in spirit. Meanwhile, there are some cords that just cannot be cut, but must be resolved first, like karma. A Maharishi once described life as being like a fever and karma as its remedy. I took this to mean that when I feel like I'm on fire, I'm burning up karmas. Burning karma is the ultimate cord cutting machete, as when it takes up residence, it burns down the whole house and we have to build a new one. We might sit around in the ashes and cry

for a while, but eventually we'll have to get up and find a new spot to build on. It's all part of the game where we come to be the witness, so the experiences don't own us. Not being owned by anything, under any circumstance is the ultimate freedom.

We've all arrived with the panacea, the antidotes for all the difficulties and hellish experiences that happen. Instead of backing away from adversity, we must extract our cure-all from it. We must cut the cords on everything that stops us from passing through the karmic flames to get to self-love and heroic action. The Good Witch takes her machete seriously; she knows what's necessary and what's not worth it. She cuts accordingly, knowing that grace demands all sorts of actions. One of these actions is to listen for the truth; when we stop all the chatter and just listen, we begin to hear it. All things speak, and when we learn the language of what things are saying, our words become powerful enough to engage or release anything. The way that the Good Witch knows what's what is that she examines all possible outcomes and they tell her. She sees karma as a spiritual sisterhood that's on board with cutting cords alongside her by exposing what's in the fire—and once she sees what isn't good enough, she lets it burn.

ENTITIES
Vanquishing Harmful Presences

"Since all the bees in the garden are buzzing around,
I'm reminded that I too am buzzing;
and though bees sting when bothered,
my most honed weapon is kindness."

Imagine if I told you your deceased grandmother was attached to your auric field. Reason being is that she was not ready to depart this world when her time came. Maybe another reason is she was so connected to you that she didn't want to leave you, so she hung around. She's actually hanging out in your energy field, using your zing as fuel to remain here while influencing you in odd ways with her old outmoded ideas. As a result, you crave foods you don't really like, act prudishly when you want to be wilder and feel mostly exhausted by six o'clock. You might feel like old Nana is close to you, she is, she's right there in your auric field enjoying your life with you!

Okay, this is just an example, because grandmothers usually become angels rather quickly when they depart, since they're

geared to support us in a protective and guiding way from heaven. Grandparents are usually not needy, they are givers. Entities are needy, as many times they are lost souls who have vampire energy and need to attach to a human in order to live. Believe me, I know about ghosts from wandering around in old houses and feeling their fleeting spirits flit around me. Some are very charming and kind, while others are mad that they're not here, so they're annoying and demand attention.

I once sold a grand 1800's home that a friend grew up in. A sea captain once owned this home and as a child, my friend constantly saw ghosts there. They weren't scary, just there. This home was in my friend's family for over fifty years, and when both her parents passed on in the house at different times, she decided it was the right time to let it go. After her father died, my friend said he was there guarding the house and would not allow what he considered the wrong types to live there. I sold it to a couple who were famous and had front-page issues, but oddly enough the house sat empty for twelve more years, no one ever moved in. My friend kept saying it was her father's doing. In due time, the house went back on the market, and once again, sat un-sold for a very long time. Eventually, it did sell because my friend said her father finally found good people. Can a relative who has passed on really control a sale? We both felt he did, and we always smiled about it.

On another note, can an entity really do evil? Well, when we're weak they can cause havoc, freak us out and jangle our nervous systems. If you ever get a feeling of *This isn't me,*

you're probably right, and you're being influenced by a needy entity. Negative entities love being influential in our wrong decisions. They send chills up our spine, leaving us confused, and then use our energy, displacing us with a lack of life-force. They're attracted to light-filled beings in the way that mosquitoes flock to light bulbs. It's useless to deny that there's dark energy out there, or that other humans may be jealous of us, wish us harm, and enjoy knocking us down. In truth, even though there are many possessed folks around, in a light-filled state, we're able to defend ourselves.

The remedies and antidotes are to constantly check our vibrations while elevating them. As the saying goes: *Trust God, but tie your camel to a tree,* meaning we must protect, clear, and constantly smudge our spaces and ourselves. And when the fake gypsies read our fortune to tell us we're cursed and we need to give them money to remove bad energy, know that they are entities incarnate. The concept of dealing with entities is simple: Scan your field to see if there's anything hanging around that isn't you, and don't freak out if there is, just surround it in a ball of light, open a vortex into the heavens and send it there—that's where it belongs anyway.

Wisely, when coming across evil people, understand they are possessed. It's discerning to send them blessings then seal your auric field; I throw light bombs on them and quickly move on. This means: Don't enmesh while reading about them in the news or watching them on television or hearing about them through the grapevine. It's most important to not hook into

any hate, even when others are wallowing in it. Hate is its own entity that goes viral, and once we begin to feel its poison, we must cleanse ourselves of it. In the same way that we bathe, we constantly have to disinfect ourselves of the negative because what we give our power to becomes more powerful. I don't believe that curses work, or nature intended us to be ill, punished, or miserable. I believe that darkness is not one millimeter as powerful as light. Therefore, when we're instilled in what is more luminous, we become secured in it.

In thinking about kindness as my most honed weapon, it is many times in kindness to myself that I consider the options and take the path that works in my interest. This is not always the easiest path, but it is the way of mastery. Like when I know in my gut that I'm wrong about my thinking and have to come to terms with myself, or when I have to apologize and consider what I need to do better. It's not easy when we're lost in negative thought forms and have to clear them to see beyond our nose; it's challenging. Especially when we have to be kind to people who are unkind—that's the hardest one of all.

Kindness is compassion in action that lets us see truths without reactions and shows us where a healing is needed. Remember everyone is going through something even if they're in denial, even when they look like they have it all going on, even when they're the expert of the moment. We're all humans juggling and clearing our shit a.k.a negative thought forms, and whoever is not doing this work is no longer any of our business. Even if you slip into a dark

hole, or are attacked by a dark entity, just hold light, keep clearing yourself, and move on.

Awareness calls for recognizing negative thought forms as an entity that's telling us lies and instilling hopelessness that causes us to mishap. So, if you feel a mood swing coming on, know it's not coming from a soul source and disperse it. Keep throwing all low-level shit up into the vortex, cry it out, immerse in a hot salt bath, and start dreaming the otherwise. Considering that we're in a mind game where the only way to get through it is to be mindful of the game—we watch our attentions and hone them in with intentions. So, while the wild west of dark times is circling, we can't be included in its shenanigans.

Here's a crazy thought: Even the Lottery is an entity. Well, not exactly the Lottery itself, but the energy around it and what it can bring out. I figured this out when I bought a ticket and got depressed that I didn't have one winning number. I next found myself scolding God for not handing over a whirlwind of money to me. Total insanity. I then sunk into all these motifs around my not being worthy to win. More craziness! Graciously, my higher perspective jumped in to say, "*Wake up! You didn't lose the Power Ball, you just contributed to someone else's win.*" This thought snapped me out of my mood swing to make me realize that we can still play in the amusement park—though it's best done from our witness perch.

I consider ego an entity, being the greatest teacher on illusion one could ever find. My ego once kidnapped me; she

tumbled my values and made excuses for my insane behaviors. Luckily Hell was not a permanent habitat and what little light I had in me at the time, expanded and saved me. Not seeing the darkness as an enemy swells our inner power so that we can walk through the shadows and remain in our light zone. I was scared to the bones when I fell into darkness, but once I acknowledged it was just an energy field, I disempowered it by thinking light-filled thoughts, so evil had nothing further to attach to.

Since darkness exists in many unexpected places, it's best to surround your living space in radiance, make a salt circle, or just as powerful, make an imaginary circle of salt around your home, your bed, your car, your pets, and your loved ones. Always bless your space, wherever you are, even on an airplane, and especially in crowds if you have to be in one. We are responsible to hold our own, so it doesn't matter what the running analogy is—we decide. When it's hard to define what's going on, keep changing your perspective until you have the one that vibrates in the highest way you can muster. As light workers, we instill harmony into discord by contributing to bring conflict into balance.

Darkness may send a sudden chill where your arm hairs stand on end, so feel around to see if there's a lost spirit or dark energy hanging around and surround it in light. I call forth their angelic ancestors to welcome them home and then open a vortex and release the entities into it. I have taken entities off my pets when they were fighting with each other for no reason and I've sent many lost spirits home to

the heavens. I have escorted deceased relatives back to their angelic tribes, I've even cleared department stores upon entering them. Imagine if shamans went into detention centers to do clearings. We are all shamans of sorts, even untrained, as our hearts know what to do. Still, with all the bad juju flying everywhere, there are many light beings around clearing the energy fields, and since you're now aware of this aspect–you're one of the scintillating cleaning crew.

Trickster concerns meanwhile are having their heyday and so it's best to stay in our heart centers and hang out in the light arenas as retaliation. These are fluctuating times where great transformations are taking place and there's no getting away with anything other than the highest accord. The darkness is being revealed to be healed, so don't see it as the enemy, see it as a friend who needs help. There's no choice other than to address these dark circumstances as hidden opportunities that need clearing. Meanwhile we're highly supported by Divine Intelligence to be doing these healings and so whatever our jobs or our paths, know that we're really super-heroes being called to uphold humanity and offer goodness to our planet.

Empowered as the new medicine beings of this world, we came here for this. I'm a Good Witch who no longer hides or pussyfoots around and is immersed in a curative plan, while Bad Bitch is on board with an ethereal bullhorn telling these entities where to go. Have you noticed that everything is being exposed? Fake news is being revealed. It's because we

have woken up and cleared the air around what to believe and have taken a stand on what we will no longer tolerate.

Consider the #MeToo movement that empowers women to call out shit on men whose lower chakras have gone out of whack. So yes, call it all out, define it and target it—though in the end always send light into it. I'm regularly smudging the energy fields around myself. I carry charged crystals in my pockets that hold my intentions. I wear amulets that affirmatively block negative energy, and many times I become invisible. Becoming invisible is fun, try it in a restaurant and see how the waiters ignore you, then turn yourself back on and see how they come to the table. This is a great way to avoid dealing with people you don't want to cross paths with. I can walk right by someone and they won't even notice I passed. I once sat on a bench in my town in an invisible manner, just to recharge and a fellow almost sat on my lap. Becoming invisible is a great way to deter entities. I do it when I enter old houses for my real estate work. I also take imaginary waterfall clearing showers, ten seconds as a mental cleanse does wonders.

One of the most powerful healing centers that I visit regularly does not actually exist on this earth plane. I walk down a path through a forest to an ornate, dome-shaped building and lay on a warm, cushioned table, surrounded by healing deities who are miracle workers. I ask for a healing and lay there in a totally peaceful state and when I'm done being healed, I feel totally light and lively. Our healings do come first on a subliminal plane and then our physical being

adapts to the alignment. Therefore, our state of mind must check into the *I Believe Healing Zone,* and we must implant this belief along with some happiness (even when we have to act as if) into our emotional auric field.

Entities are not like implants in the sense of being thought forms we buy into, they are lost spirits that are wandering, or purposely hanging around. At this stage of the game their energy can pass through social media, television, the news, and other people. An entity that sends out fear is snaking into our nervous system while triggering emotions to take us down. Anger is a reaction to these attacks, while extended sadness and depression are soul disconnections. Emotions have layers that when triggered, go into thought forms with controlling aspects to kidnap and disempower us. During these spells where a mood grabs us, just consider where in ourselves we agreed to be part of it and disown it.

The truth is that dark stuff is constantly flying around, though it can only attach to and affect a frequency of its like kind. The way you undermine it is by being aware and determined in handling it. Holding a higher state is repellent to entities, as they will try all their tricks to poison us and once we turn on our lights—they flee. A friend who has occasional migraine version anxiety attacks told me she got one as she walked through a shit storm without her raincoat. She wasn't taking care of herself. In other words, during these tumultuous times, what our destiny boils down to is about how we're moving into mastery. Disarming dark energy is easy when we skillfully have the intention to do so,

and now that we're aware of entities and dark energy, the skills are at hand.

I recently moved into a building on a beach as a winter escape and found some of the other tenants to be opinionated. I then realized that people with judgement issues put themselves on pedestals and it's none of my business. They gossip and create cliques and like to have us-and-them scenarios. For me, this winter retreat is a sacred healing place, so I decided to hold myself in a Holy state above their scenarios. In the face of abjection, we're here to be the ones who are not lost in worldly mindsets—we can Jujitsu energy fields while we're in the world, but not in the darkness of it.

I love the concept of *Who do you think you are?* Who we think we are is just our ego trying on personalities. Who we really are is a God-Force in operation, a gleam of magic in the moment, love in action. There are so many things to be besides who we think we are—like being super-heroes who are in service to the highest good. As a magical entity having a human experience, sometimes we do battle to avoid getting lost in a fear-based overstory. The Bad Bitch, when she goes off her emotional grid, gets lost in her own mind and is constantly attacked by entities. In her nasty zone, she has a bull's eye target on her back that says, "*Hit me!*" The Good Witch is always on hand to help Bad Bitch get back up while she pulls out the arrows. Good Witch is an enterprise of valuable perspective with vivid imaginary powers that transcend darkness.

We might consider Bad Bitch an emotional entity, though

she's actually one of our warriors in training. A trained bitch is a powerful asset: she is patient and waits for weak spots to be revealed. No longer throwing a punch, she laughs and walks away when people turn against her. Their punishment is their loss of her, even if they don't know it. Relieved that she is free of them, she thanks the Universe for their removal, because she trusts the hello/goodbye seasons in life. Granted, she might slip here and there because she's not afraid to learn from her mistakes and is up on self-forgiveness as a daily activity. This is a being who owns her shit, no longer throws it around, stays clear of drama, and stands her ground. Even entities are leery of hanging around reformed Badass Bitches—especially psychic ones with Good Witch alliances.

Dealing with Entities

- Scan the energy of people that you come in contact with prior to enmeshing with them. Negative people are viral with entities.
- I have asked argumentative people who I do business with, to please put their higher selves on the phone line. They hang up on me, so that's one way to get rid of them.
- Sometimes we need to deal with these difficult types and can't get out of it. Like a nasty secretary at the doctor's office, or a mean airline representative on the phone. Consider them God in a bad mood and

try to cheer them up—just don't hook into their mood.

- We are an entity escort service that steadily guides lost spirits into their best realms, so routinely scan yourself and loved ones for unnecessary spirit matter and send all unwanted presences into the light.
- Clear all your emotional scars, as they attract energy of a like kind.
- Become a blank slate; this clears negative storylines.
- Leaving an open space creates a void that invites the Universe to step in.
- Empower your radiance by being light-filled.
- Don't invest in evil, instead open a vortex and send it in to disperse and heal.
- Samskara: the Sanskrit definition of impressions that solidify our conditioning. Negative samskaras reinforce self-lacerating mental patterns that absolutely hinder our evolution, so the antidote is positive conditioning.
- A negative entity is an astral being with *samskaras* that needs to be cleansed. Remind them and tell them you are healing them before sending them off.
- Remember, reality is make-believe made manifest
- In the land of make-believe, we choose how it goes.
- Stay Holy in all that you do.
- Face the unknown knowing that you're able to send light into any reality.
- Instill life force into new patterns.

- Be aware, instead of holding a "*Beware*" vibe.
- Remember that we're witch doctors who mend energy fields.
- Be gentle and loving when dealing with entities; it disorients them.
- Shamans trap entities in a crystal and release them from there. I wave feathers over them and send them into a light vortex, which is done in my imagination—a most powerful tool.
- Drama is a sign that negative entities are active, so when loved ones go out of whack and try to drag me in, I pull back and do a healing on their cosmic field. I call in their good spirit to help and they usually come back into harmony within hours.
- Always clear and protect yourself first; we can't help others when we are not clear.
- We have the tools and defense modes needed for these times. We also have instant access into our child-mind that makes up our magical armory. It was a child-mind that created my imaginary entity vacuum hose that pulls off entities and shoots them into to the heavens to be dealt with.
- Our imaginary concepts are unlimited.
- Believe that you have the power, for as the Good Witch told Dorothy at the Emerald Palace in the Land of Oz: "*You had the power all along my dear.*"
- Get out your ruby slippers—or star-studded combat boots—and own your empowered self.

FORGIVENESS
Compassionate Clemency

"In the turnaround to love, we no longer hold resentments, while love clears the poison."

Another realtor in my office spit in my face. We were both looking at a vacant space for rent when we had a disagreement, and she spit. She was immediately fired. And as she walked out the door, she looked at me with steely eyes and said she would get me, so watch out. I believed her, so I watched my back, especially when turning corners in the supermarket. Amusingly, she called me a year later asking me to help her to get back into the business. She wanted a desk at the new company where I worked. I quickly forgave her with no hesitation. I did it because I was tired of watching my back and I'm attracted to forgiveness.

Here is the conversation my Bad Bitch had with my higher self . . .

Higher Self: You must forgive Elizabeth! (Name changed.)

Me: Never!

Higher Self: This is not a request. It's a mandatory requirement.

Me: Are you making me?

Higher Self: Yes, and you must do it for real.

Me: Ok Elizabeth, I forgive you.

Ten minutes later . . .

Me: Wow, I feel so good.

Higher Self: Right: you didn't do it for her, you did it for you.

Shit's always flying around; we live in a crowded world surrounded by agendas. When you know the secret—that it's not about them, or who did what, or all that's streaming—then you will know it's about our relationship with life and nothing else. This relationship is the conversation that reflects our reality back to us. Bad Bitch has moments of inner hysteria when things go wrong, though you'd never know it because she goes stone-faced and does an immediate inner retreat. She's learned that confrontations give her the opportunity to attain mastery. Sinking into the quicksand of negativity is one path, though every time we're battered, we must turn things around to find that even the worst situations have a few good angles and once we find the intersection the worst situation will turn a corner. It doesn't mean the worst situations are okay, it means that we're going to be okay.

A panoramic vision to see the obverse is needed to bring

the better way into sight. An example is: I got caught up in the whirlwind of a friend's wound when she tried to blame me for a trigger. The first alert is we've rolled into a defense mode. I then saw myself coming up with arguments around why it wasn't my fault. Pulling myself back and looking at the bigger picture, I realized this was an ego dispute that had nothing to do with me, so I withdrew my ego. My friend then realized that her argument was about a pattern within herself—not with me. It's our responsibility to define our own ways, our projections, and to deal with our emotions until we get to what for we are giving. Meaning what is the reasoning around what we give our energy to—and what's the end result we wish to end up with?

A domino effect became apparent when a client's husband questioned my integrity after I told him he needed to reduce the price of his house and he refused. His wife responded by immediately agreeing and then questioned her husband's integrity for not agreeing when he originally agreed to do whatever it takes to sell their home quickly. When we don't feel a need to defend ourselves, we see how what we say about others translates to the fact that we are only ever talking about ourselves. An elderly client called me difficult. I can be difficult, but he was clearly defining himself. I told his house manager, who told me that he called her difficult too, meanwhile she is a sweetheart of a woman. Funny how the accusations that get flung clearly describe the characterizations of what we're dealing with, so when a hot potato is flung, don't catch it. We must take care

of ourselves by not taking on shit that's not ours—and if it's really ours to deal with, we must roll up our sleeves, put our ego in timeout, and deal.

What if you hurt me and I let you get away with it? You did something so inexcusable, so filled with betrayal, that it caused me severe pain. My immediate response was to get back at you, to tell everyone, and to make you suffer the way you made me. My Bad Bitch is expert at striking back but today, when you damaged me, I went to my corner, curled into a ball and felt every millimeter of the pain. I then called forth my ambulatory angels and together we healed my wounds. When I looked back at you, all I saw were aspects of an old version of myself that no longer existed.

We've all done inexcusable things, saying things we could not take back. We've lost it in a rage, made excuses and looked the other way when we were needed. It's not about thinking *so what*. The excuse of *so what* is a slip-slide into a mindset that makes up rules based on convenience instead of virtue. We know when we're being challenged to do the right thing; that little feeling inside poking our *This is Wrong* button. When we're pulled to go amiss, telling ourselves we can get away with it, it's bullshit, we don't ever get away with it. Not going down that road is our saving grace, or if we've gone down it, owning it and making amends is our other saving grace.

I was recently asked by a friend, who wanted to be paid for a lead, to do something many brokers in my business do. It was to call a man whose wife just died to get his real estate listing. I

refused. My friend said: "All the other top brokers would do it." The test was not to judge her, but to have compassion for her judgments. She wanted me to get that listing and pay her a referral on it. We've all been desperate, indulging in dark aspects even just in thought. We must own desperation and every other crappy motivation we've considered. By and large we've all experienced every torturously horrific level of mental, emotional and physical suffering that's ever existed. We've witnessed hell in our lifetimes, while some of us have lost everything, including our families. The heartbreak of these stories still resounds in the ethers, waiting to be healed. All things that cause disturbance and pain are issues calling for mending. What we are repairing is not the circumstance itself, but the deep-seated feelings we carry around it–especially the grief.

Desperation is really about a lack of deserving; it grabs for things, acting out of lack, and knocking down our integrity. In retaliation, the Universe then pulls back on delivering abundance, as we get exactly what we're in alignment with. I'd have loved to list that house but would never impose on someone's period of grief. I always ask myself, is this the right thing to do? We know the truth and we know when things are not right.

The truth is that we're now in a chronology where what we do, feel, and say, really counts. There is a general responsibility revolving around our actions, so we can no longer go with the status quo. It does not matter what others think is okay, only that little voice inside that needs to be

heard matters. The Good Witch is always talking to herself on the higher bandwidth; she knows the little voice is her highest alliance and guide that's always channeling messages.

It takes courage not to do the easy thing, to go the other way, to change how we roll. Right now, the universe is birthing a new breed of beings who are doing very sacred work by holding an evolved state of being. Their energy is contagious and while we might not know these beings personally, when our awakening is ripe, we're affected by them. In the interim, we might feel suffocated and pushed around from still fighting the flow, but once we go with it we're coming out as new versions of ourselves. In the past, I would have gone for that listing but I'm no longer that person with that agenda, and the goodness that rolls in is so scintillatingly blissful it goes beyond what money can buy.

Helen Keller once said, "It is wonderful how much time good people spend fighting the devil. If they would only expend the same amount of energy loving their fellowmen, the devil would die in his own tracks of ennui." Imagine sending the wrong doers some love, throwing some love bombs their way. This doesn't mean we agree with them, it means we are healers rising above animosity. The saying: "*Let he who is free from sin cast the first stone,*" reminds us that no one's exempt from a dark side–acknowledge it. Darkness by itself doesn't come from other people, countries, or enemies, it lives in our own minds. In order for darkness to exist, it has to have a like-kind form to attach itself to, so the shadows that surround us are directives that show us where

to shine our light. When our dark side is brought into the light, we have mercy. Mercy is compassion for the enemy, an act that brings divine favor along with a blessing.

A truck driver sped up and tried to cut me off as I went to pull out of a parking space. I was quick and pulled out anyway, meeting the trucker at the next light. He spewed curses at me for making him brake, so I told him he had two choices: one was to let me in, in which case I would be saying thank you and wishing him a nice day, or this curse-fest he was having. Interesting that we were stopped at the light, being a metaphoric place to pause and think about how and where we're going. The trucker again chose to spew more curses, and I chose to wish him a nice day anyway. My nasty bitch would have cursed him back and sent him off with a whammy hex, but Good Witch sent him sincere blessings and threw him some love bombs. My reactor did not even tick, which is not to say I'm always this elevated, though my clean-up crew is on it when I'm not. There are days that I have to get off my high broom and start sweeping as I say, many times: "I'm so sorry." The difference between my nasty bitch and my Good Witch is, I mean it.

Every time we react, fight back, or gossip, we lose power. Our worst defeat comes when we lose the good feeling we have about ourselves because we're not proud of our actions. It's an addiction to react and go for the jugular and it takes a commitment to break down the rational and lies we tell ourselves about how it's okay to be that way. We must get beyond vindication for our higher reasoning to become a

directive, as when we don't empower antagonism and by healing what's hurting us, we're alleviating darkness and advocating for peace.

My mother and her older sister used to fight, holding grudges that lasted years. The sad part was that my mother really loved this sister and sincerely wanted to heal their rift. Their last argument was so meaningless that even we, being the cousins, had no idea what it was about. On my mother's deathbed, she called out again and again for her sister to come and make peace with her. My Aunt never came, she never called, she never showed up at the funeral, and she forbade her children to attend. Not a card or a flower was ever sent. I wanted to scream, "*WAKE UP*" at the top of my lungs, but all I could do was wake up for them. Now that all four of the sisters are gone, all the cousins who remain sincerely love each other. It's as if we've survived some historic dark dynamic that ended with the Aunts who procured it.

In the days when my Bad Bitch was on her high horse, things culminated in an explosion at the real estate brokerage where I worked. I threw all my things in a Hefty bag and sat on the sidewalk in Bridgehampton, figuring out what to do next. I had quit, though my manager said I was fired and then tried to blackball me everywhere. She stole all my listings and tarnished my already edgy reputation as best she could. I survived and was welcomed by a woman who owned a new company which became the largest real estate agency on the East Coast. Once again, as the decade-long top producer of this new company, I forgave my old manager. I

still loved her for her great training, even though she tried to slay me. To this day, I call her for her expertise as what happened is behind us because my light side forgave her dark side and we both moved on. In the act of forgiving others, we forgive ourselves.

I once spent a period of time at a meditation ashram in upstate New York. While the talks and meditations were free, people made offerings at the end of the evening to support the programs. There was one wealthy family who always attended, and one day while everyone was meditating, their teenage son was caught in the coat room stealing money from coat pockets. The family was at their wits' end with their troubled boy. Finally, they were called to a meeting with the head of the ashram, who decided that this boy would have the job of counting all the money donated at the end of every weekend. The family was shocked. Mind you, the ashram drew hundreds of people, so it was substantial money. The message the master gave the boy was that she trusted him to change and this changed him. I think of this whenever I'm mad at myself, when I've screwed up, when I could've done better–and I then trust myself to do so.

Nasty Bitch had a sorry-/not-sorry attitude, while Good Witch is truly sorry for former mistakes, but has zero guilt because she's owned her lessons. Concurrently, Good Witch regards Bad Bitch as a sacred character in our tale and has no desire to annihilate her or put her down. It's the part of us that believes in our greatness that inspires it to come out.

Bad Bitch is now on a team to be reckoned with, for when our devil and angel unite, we become divinely transformed into living archangels.

A friend who loves to eradicate lesser personages in herself and others, thinks that when she identifies these dispositions, she can then call them out and *snap*–they disappear. It doesn't work like that, at least not for me. I have to dance with them, feel their moves, get into the soul of them. I have to go low with them in order to heal with them. I've learned this the hard way, as you can't just know better. Yes, we should know better, but we don't until we do. And in order to know better, we really have to know to the bones what's *not* better. We put our hand in the fire, we cry in pain, and we heal–that's how we know.

My niece Kenza was a powerful force who inherited a definitive edgy influence from my mother, along with her addictions. The moment our eyes met, I knew her power was huge, and even in her childhood she knew how to use it. We used to fight. At three years old, she would run ahead into a restaurant, grab the best seat at the table and refuse to move. I was impressed by the way she always knew where the best spot was. Our fights were power struggles and she always won because she knew my weak spots and would poke them. As a teenager, she had my wild edge and I adored her for it, yet we fought even more.

The last time I saw her alive was five years ago, when she came to visit me, just out of drug rehab. We laid on my bed and watched *Orange is the New Black*. I yelled at her about her

vape smoke as it was making me cough; she said it wasn't doing that. I said it was toxic; she said it wasn't. She perused my medicine cabinet and stole my husband's abandoned pain pills, prescribed for his broken leg surgery. I wondered why she slept for days; she was bonked-out on drugs *again*. We fought over that too. I gave her a suitcase full of designer clothes and we fought over a Pucci top I wanted to keep, she won. She wanted to leave early; I wanted her to stay. She twisted the experience of that visit around, which made me look bad to her mom. She was basically falling apart, and I was too angry to get it. I wish I could have a do-over. I wish I could have helped her, listened, and understood. I feel like I failed her, but even more so, I failed myself as I loved her so much yet could not be there for her.

She died at twenty-three from a Fentanyl overdose. I don't think she meant to die; it was a hard week and after eight months of being clean, one slip and she was gone. Flying to Los Angeles, I wrote the eulogy I would share at her funeral; it was titled *Forgiveness.* Stunned and in shock, I was asking her what to say as we passed through the clouds. I heard one word loud and clear: Forgiveness. The eulogy I wrote was about how she always came back to love, no matter what, and that's where I would find her. I thought the message I received meant to forgive her for leaving. I was wrong. It meant that I should forgive myself for my perceived failure in not helping her. Not a day goes by that I don't think of her and realize what I might have done better. She was a teacher, a sister, a force to reckon with. In the end, her presence, here

and there, smacked me so hard it woke me up to be a better person for her.

Even as a child, my niece would turn and look at me when I was in my nasty bitch mode and in an adult penetrating voice she'd say, *Stop it, Tati!* (Tati, an endearing word for *Tante*, means Aunt in French, which Kenza spoke fluently.) Shit, I was so proud of her, and now here I am forgiving myself because that's her gift to me. Still I would crawl for a re-do, for a chance to listen better, to understand her pain, to hug her one more time. In a mental re-do, I've done things a bazillion times over in my mind and I know she knows. It's time for self-forgiveness, and it's a private affair between us and who we are in spirit. Spirit tells me that we're now complete and to just stay in love, as that's what Kenza would want. If her presence ever impacted anyone or anything, the message would be: *Love Is All That Matters*! This message is my bottom line; the place I go to when a confrontation exists.

While our hearts break daily over the hardships we witness, there's infinite mercy in the fact that we're here doing what we do, as we evolve through our struggles. Our hearts know when to call out for a healing of all that's hurting us, they know more than our minds. In order to follow our heart, we first have to open it, let it bleed, let its ecstasy come through, and then listen to its message. The universe then meets us at a heart level and together we beat the drum of love that continues to pulse in all realms for eternity—as the nature of Hearts is For Giving!

Compassionate Forbearing

- Excuses are indolent ideas in the way of owning our shit.
- We have to remove the ego implant from our vision to see truth.
- The truth may be harsh, but like medicine, it attacks what doesn't belong.
- Shortcomings remind us to turn and face the mirror, as the reflection out there is ours.
- We forgive because it releases us from being imprisoned by our own bad feelings.
- A wound is really an alarm that says: *Address This Issue Now!*
- The wounds we carry are not our crosses to bear—they're past crises up for recovery.
- To beg a pardon is not to beg to differ, it's to be reprieved.
- The only argument worth having is one that has a loving solution.
- The act of reprievable compassion brings amnesty.
- We become stronger by not holding on to what is lesser.
- Love is a shape shifter, turning an awful experience into one that inspires gratitude.
- The Jujitsu of amity brings discord into harmony.
- A grudge is false power and a judgment that does not hold higher understanding.

- Self-forgiveness is self-love in action.
- What we overlook has less influence than what we love—look for love.
- Choosing to love beyond altercations doesn't mean the feud is okay, it means we choose love over it and are invested in where it goes.
- When it's time to hash things out, step forward. When shit is being flung, step back.
- There's nothing that can't be healed in our mind's eye.
- Seeing the bigger picture is about investing in the better storyline.
- Sometimes love means rolling up your sleeves and working your ass off for togetherness.
- There are big lessons in what's not easy—once we get them, things become easier.
- Forgiveness is disentanglement from our own darkness.
- Regret is the teacher who uses our own actions as the spanking.
- It's fine to love difficult people and not have dinner with them.
- Don't argue with adversaries—throwing love bombs and walking away is enough.
- A genius motivation is never stop trying to go higher with yourself.
- Forgiveness does not delete the issue, it heals it.

- The moment you think of revenge, think of forgiveness as the revenge against revenge.
- Forgiveness is the twin of understanding.
- Self-examination is not for weaklings, it has wings.
- Own your shit and use it to compost something better.
- Since everything is an opportunity, we greet opposition with a peace sign.
- Even in protest, we can yell in the name of peace.
- Consider the concept of bringing yourself to peace and then do what it takes.
- All the relationships we're having go back to how we relate to ourselves.
- Nothing will be satisfying until we get comfortable within ourselves.
- Our best memories draw us back to who we are in our soul, to enhance us.
- The difference between understanding and forgiveness is that understanding has legs, while forgiveness has wings.
- Make good memories often, look to the light of things, and know you're here For Giving.
- In the end. . . *LOVE is all that Matters!*

PART TWO

RITUALS & CEREMONY

"The Pow-Wow for what is sacred is to be performed
alone with spirit, in a group,
in a dream, in a vision, in a made-up tale,
in a creation of choice, or
as an ordinance to confirm trust, alleviate pain,
create abundance, release emotion,
bring joy, honor grace–and to affirm whatever the heck is needed."

I woke up to honor the highest aspects in myself during a time when my lowest aspects were raging. I began to live in ceremony using daily rituals to honor my process. In the festive ways that we come together with our loved ones on holidays, living this life as a sacred ceremony holds events of ritual significance that honor our occasion. Akin to the sacrament of marriage, where we stand before God and pledge our alliance to another, or at the passing of a loved one where we commune with others in honoring their life, we are formally offering our hearts in sacred ritual and asking the Gods for blessings. In these times, we must esteem transformation as we are now part of the movement of darkness toward light.

Since there are many illusions running to distract us from being powerful, we're continually side-tracked. Ceremony and rituals escort us back into our power and solidify our standing. The question is where are we standing and what are we standing for? When I lost myself in the folly of being a nasty bitch, it was a very back-and-forth time where I fluctuated between good and evil by trying to be a better person. It's bullshit to try to be a better person, as the desire for enhancement is a state of consciousness, not a way of being. Honoring ourselves for being here as courageous adventurers in these tumultuous times makes us valued persons, even if just to ourselves. We are standing at the pivot point of a sacred turnaround whose goal is to merge us into oneness with our inner power place. This sacred inner world says: *Life is our ceremony and our rituals are how we live it.*

The berth from where we define what's valid is a place of divine creativity. Here we bow to our inner warrior in a ceremony that honors our fierce standing, which esteems how we've survived trauma, how we've learned from harsh lessons and how we hold our own. Honoring ourselves is a dynamic undertaking; it is stating that even while we're down, hanging out in harsh realities that don't support our morale, we recognize our great spirit behind us, and in the blink of remembrance–we're one with them. When I fell off my high horse, I wandered through my forest lost until I tapped into my Good Witch within. She did a soul retrieval on me, a welcome home ritual that embraced me back to my gameness, which reminded me of my stoutheartedness. By

reconnecting to who we are in spirit, we hone into our natural pulse, which pushes us to reach through a bevy of imposed personas to grab ourselves back to our true selves.

I thought I had to be nice in order to burn karma. Wrong! I had to be real and sometimes real doesn't feel at all nice. Sometimes real is scared to the bones and from here we confront, we summon valor, and do the breakthrough dance in alliance with our essential spirit. It's not always pretty, our descent to retrieve ourselves. We face the monster with endless heads, and for a while we slay them, but the heads keep coming back until we embrace the reflection of what their expression is and where in ourselves, we mirror it. Accepting where we are is the turnaround that turns us in all directions until we stop fighting, making excuses, analyzing, and choose to cradle our bad selves. By recognizing all aspects of who we are, we heal.

I was speaking with my son, who was describing his perception of the quality of the world these days, which was quite dark. We have a natural instinct to want to fix things when sometimes all we can do is listen. He was describing intense levels of discomfort around the crash-and-burn quality of life that the pandemic brought out and described the social protocols running and the prior demands to fit into them or fail. He felt compelled to be creative to support himself while feeling totally lost. I was trying to share solutions to relieve his discomfort, when he forcefully told me to Stop It! He said, "I *should* feel uncomfortable around these issues, I should feel damn uncomfortable." He was right, there was nothing

satisfying happening. He owned his unease in a rightful manner and was using it to move himself in another direction. In this sense, being real is a transformer that uses discomfort as a propellant.

Things change when we're being squeezed to grow out of what no longer works. The voice within says: *Fear is a test to find the essence inside us that we need in order to come forth to face it.* As in the daily ritual of deciding what to wear, which expresses our frame of mind, we must peruse our emotions for the keys to our empowerment. Life is a ritual of seasons, each one offering an invitation to gain mastery. Heartbreak is the season of embracing ourselves, the interval to heal and come back stronger. Transformation, being the season of change, bears the message that we're dropping loads of what we no longer need. The ceremony around these revisions is not to back away from the unfamiliar but to trust the unknown as a magical domain and enter it with respect in awe of its hidden gifts.

We're being forced to think outside the box and it's with curiosity that we summon the balls to venture out from the same old ways. Our conviction has a vein that embraces us to dance with new possibilities. Confidence has a say-so that states: *It doesn't matter what anyone else thinks, doesn't matter if there's rejection, doesn't matter if we can't find the input for our output, because we're following a new pulse with its own rhythm.* Conviction grabs us to blow through minefields of opposition as faith carries us when we can't walk. The euphoria in this dance attracts our new dance partners because it moves us. Think

about the word *Because* and apply it to *Being the Cause* of what matters most. It then matters not if we arrive, as all that matters is how we feel as we go.

Concurrently, it's time to relish the daily things that give us respite, including even the ritual of making a cup of coffee. In the simple act of paying homage to what we cherish, our gratitude is our good fortune that becomes magnified. We must ritualize everything from a necessary forgiveness to energizing dreams on the new moon. Ritualize your wares (your marketable commodity) as an offering. Ritualize your contemplations and make room for them, be open to what they bring when they're honored. Consider the infiniteness of vastness and then acknowledge the absoluteness we've arrived here from. Sometimes on the hour, I have to take a moment of reverie to clear my mind from collective overload and reconnect to my heart. This kind of contemplation automatically pulls me into an elevated state where the smallness of a condition broadens into a grander frame of reference.

An example is I was in a disagreement with my son and all my buttons were pushed. I was livid and went to the beach to contemplate my next move. I had gotten off the phone without continuing to argue, but was not resolved. Sitting on the beach, rolling through my anger, suddenly higher reasoning came through and said: *Walk your talk.* The moment I recognized a better way existed, I ritualized it by putting it on a pedestal and bowing to it. I honored that I trusted it to work for me and in doing so, within a short period the anger was gone, the phone rang, it was my son and we worked it out.

By ritualizing our quality of life, it's mandatory to transform bad feelings, fears, and obsessive thinking, because it matters more that we place our focus in the reality we want to be part of. The trick is to enhance a normal activity with a gracious state of consciousness that shifts the ordinary into the extraordinary. Shifting our energy to holding ourselves in an exhilarated state opens the way to the best symmetry. An example is that I always say a quick prayer that I not fall into a battle zone while in a confrontation. The prayer is: *May what's best for the situation preclude personal behaviors and may I have the ability to accept what doesn't work and rise above it without taking it personally.* Once I say this prayer, I'm armed and whatever happens, I'm held in an elevated state. It's the difference between asking to be elevated and making a statement that enhances elevation. The first way holds an elevated state above us while the other way slides us right into it.

During a very difficult transition where I found myself complaining and describing how awful it was, someone very close to me fell into a deep depression. Granted, many of us are going through extremely hard times and on many subliminal levels we energetically hold each other up. I had a heart-to-soul conversation with this person, which is a ceremony in itself, and I realized that I don't get to have a break on slip-sliding into a poor-me zone. It's because this person needs me and is holding me to the highest standards, so they can believe in possibility. Some of us are role models for our loved ones—it's just the way it is. We can't pass the

hot potatoes, instead we have to transform them. I've shifted patterns of falling into disappointments to preferably creating rituals of celebration that honor my attainments. It's important to congratulate ourselves as in: *It's so wonderful, my dear self, that you've realized such wisdom and I commend you for this fearless endeavor.*

How often do we celebrate our personal endeavors instead of displaying egocentric bravado? A friend has magnificent plans; he's been moving things around in preparation to make these plans happen. Sometimes though he beats himself up for the delay instead of being blissed out while moving things around and knowing that he's in perfect timing. Timing is everything, for how we live is ritually ensconced in routines that must be revered in order to deliver. If we see everyday life as part of a vast blueprint of the bigger picture, we can transcend worldly events to reach a more stellar way of being. We can also transcend the daily grind, as what looks like the "*Same Old Thing*" is really a time to let the magic behind the scenes come into motion. Trusting that magic exists and is working for us, we show up for the greater good while we take out the garbage.

On this journey, many times we have to do things we don't want to do. I took care of my mother for years when she was ill and dying. At the time she was crazier than ever, and my inner bitch wanted to put a pillow over her head. Instead, I held her hand and waited it out with her. One of my rituals is to honor what's in the dung pile, the pile we're supposed to step over or dump in the garbage. I hear inside:

There's gold in them hills and I must excavate it. Funny that every time I come across a good dung pile, how I approach it depends upon whether or not I'm impassioned in life. When I'm impassioned I find the gold easily and when I'm not I get covered in dung.

I was so impassioned at the start of my real estate career that driving around looking at houses felt ecstatic. I sang songs I made up about how rich I was, when I was actually almost broke. Every activity and every phone call made was charged with my energetic ardor. Other brokers thought I was nuts and they made fun of me, but they shut up when I became the top producer of the office in less than a year. I was living in a joyful fevered state using rituals that pulled abundance right to me. I blessed every phone call, every listing, and every buyer as being sent to me by God. Though when my nasty bitch stepped in, the dung pile got huge and I slipped off a mountain of my shit, right into it. This blunder was not solely a downslide; it was rather an expedition back from all the ways I'd lost myself.

Amazing how parts of ourselves become kidnappers and we have to free ourselves from ourselves. I was out to dinner recently when two real estate brokers sitting at the next table told me how wonderful I am these days and how a decade ago they were terrified of me. I asked them what they were afraid of and they said that they thought I would put a spell on them. It's true, back then I would have. Though what they were really afraid of was my huge uncontrolled energy as powerful thoughts are like bombs. My humanness would still love to hit

the next human in the sandbox when they grab my pail and shovel, and sometimes I still do, but only in my mind until my good spirit comes online to distract me. These days when I have bad thoughts, I sit in ceremony with them and write them out, and then I burn them while I hone into a higher understanding that transforms my feelings.

Meanwhile, nasty bitch still whispers dark innuendoes into my ear while my Good Witch grabs me back from her tricks. Hanging out in my private sanctum, a safe space where I allow my anger to come screaming out, I want to understand where this anger is coming from in order to quell it. Knowing better than to follow nasty bitch who holds my passport to Hell, I listen to her concerns to alleviate them. She once stole my passion, though I stole it back while I held her hand to make her give it up. Now she sits with me and helps me to shift the seasons in my temple, as I call on ethereal forces for support and request a rite of passage into my latest powerful Good Witch worthy decree. It's the old *give the monkey something to do* trick, as in: Listen bitch, you sit here with my basket of knitting and we're going to knit my life together in the highest way.

Bad bitch still hates cleaning, especially toilets, and tells me to hire a maid. I've tricked her again by telling her we're not cleaning but clearing the way for a huge new spell. It's not a total lie, as my bouts of cleaning are another ritual I use to clear energy. During the short period when my family and I lived in upstate New York at an ashram, I was the ashram hairstylist. I had a small salon and was doing quite

the business. It was summertime, and thousands of people would arrive to sit in meditation. One day I received a message from the meditation master saying I should collect all the hair I cut and burn it in a bonfire on the new moon to clear the karmas of the people whose hair I cut. If you've ever smelled burned hair, it stinks. I would stand in the cold mountain evenings, burning piles of hair by the light of those moons, and many times I was furious. I hated burning that hair and questioned my sanity. My inner bitch was screaming: *This is not what we signed on for!* Actually, it was a new moon ceremony I was performing to alleviate the suffering of others when I realized I was actually burning my own karma by being in service.

The Universe will give us a reflection of what's needed when it's necessary to break through issues that are holding us back from our enlightenment. I remember standing in the lobby of this ashram one weekend when a famous surgeon arrived at the front desk and was given the honored *Seva* (selfless service) of cleaning the public bathrooms. This man had a total fit, well really it was his ego that had the fit. It was obvious he arrived to sit in meditation and did not plan on cleaning toilets, but obviously he needed to clean up a bunch of shit in his life, so there he was. It was another instance of having to do things we don't believe we were meant to do. I love when this happens; it means there's a pile of gold in the shit storm around my annoyance and the game is to find it.

I once had a toilet-cleaning experience on my first job at a hair salon, when at eighteen I was immersed in my bad-bitch

self. The two lovers who owned the salon, David and Jason, were passionate, artistic, volatile men. If things were not done to perfection, there was a scene. Everything was addressed with supreme consideration from the flowers to the way one dressed. They became my new parents who gave me lessons on how to set a table, answer the phone, look at art, be elegant, and most importantly how to clean. David handed me the toilet brush on that first day. "I don't do toilets," I replied. To which he said, "Then there's the door, leave."

I cried while washing the toilet, and then we went on to lessons of how to fold towels, sweep up hair, make the best coffee ever and serve the patrons. He taught me how to scrub dirt, starting with first you had to see the dirt. I became a Sherlock grunge detective, though I was really like Cinderella on my knees scrubbing and crying that this was not what I signed up for. I was an assistant in training, instructed that everything was to be treated with extreme consideration, and to get into it as if I was being blessed by each activity. What was insane was that I needed all this behind-the-scenes training to become great at my craft, for what I was really being taught was how to observe and regard. Interestingly the salon was called Antenna and by the time I finally emerged dressed by these boys in couture on the salon floor, I was a master hairstyling goddess, though my bad bitch was still intact.

Transformation is its own ceremony that moves in its own time frame, and as far as consciousness goes, it could take years, even lifetimes to become conscious and you have

to ask for it. Otherwise we're stuck in personas like me as a nasty bad bitch and we don't evolve. When I'm struggling, I ask myself the question: *Is this worth it?* Thankfully, I transcended being only a nasty bad bitch and this is not to say I now live in Pollyanna-ville as there are still constant battles going on within. *Is it worth it?* I would not trade it for a comfortable, unchallenging life where I couldn't grow, evolve, and be in service. The Good Witch is humble; she shows gratitude for all that has been bestowed. She honors the lessons, the path, and what she can offer. Even though she still has an edge that she uses when necessary, she no longer lives in nasty bitch mode–she lives in ceremony. There's no going into ceremony—this is it!

All that's happening right now is part of the ceremony, even the struggles of this world. The Universe handing us a scrub brush is part of the ceremony, as is our getting up in the morning and how we go through the day by dealing with all that's needed. Harsh people, hideous times, catastrophes, and severe grief, all are instances that are begging to be inaugurated into better circumstances. Therefore, the rituals we perform when we're consciously in harmony around our undertakings are poignant in how they cut to the core of what's valid during such intense times. A performed ceremony is an acclimation bringing us into a higher way of being; it reminds us to go to a place of spiritual power and come from there. While rituals advocate clearings, they create a rite of doing what's necessary instead of what's easy, and they request that we commit to what's worthy over all else.

The Good Witch is always reminding me to mentally switch gears and carry myself in a sacred way, while her rituals revolve around doing what it takes to get to our holy land. During the times I'm lost in the crazy jungle slaying my own demons, I have to take it seriously that even the slaying needs to be done in a sacred way. Living a sacred existence reminds us that the way we honor life is the contribution we offer. Our difficulties, our grief, our overcoming setbacks, depression, addictions, and our transformations are all calling for offerings from us and this is the gift. The main offering is that we show up for ourselves and as such our lives are lived in ceremony to these offerings. In ceremony we hold our own hands in prayer, in fists, giving the fu*k off finger, in the peace sign, and open to receiving grace–while we do what's needed above all else to take us across.

RITUALS FOR LIFE
Homebodies . . .

"To see what is blessed, meaningful, abounding with beauty, resonating with joy, torn by a broken heart; defines our showing up as the ritual that says, I am here even to make you tea, to wake up to another day, to die, and to be part of all things great and small."

As a child, when I was told to go to my room, I was secretly thrilled. I would slide into a state of wonder, moving from daydreaming, to getting lost in books, playing with dolls, and imagining my future alliances. I was often found singing songs I made up as I lazed in dimensions of my creation. Solitude is an important time that we need to be immersed in more often than not. Under pressure is a good description of what this new age has demised, as even alone there is so much we have to do. In quarantine, we were all sent to our rooms to sit in timeout and transform every reality we were part of. Imagine it as not being a punishment, but a privilege to take a breath of clean consciousness and see how to go from there. Everything that was in process prior came to a stop and there was a reprieve on every level, even as we

thought about the lack of toilet paper and the things we take for granted.

We were not sent to our rooms, but to a sacred space to contemplate our existence and how it's really going. If we don't take a dip once in a while into our own ethereal cosmic pond, we will continue to be constantly under pressure and immersed in patterns that don't take us anywhere good. The onslaught stops when we ground into our holy zone, which of course is many times also imaginary. So, we traipse through experiences and then we come home to process them.

Crazy, I remember being a baby and considering my little body a landing pad, a home of sorts that I would come back to after hours of wondrous explorations. Now, I find myself reading energy fields, moving things around and delving into cosmic dimensions. My out-of-bounds consciousness harmonizes me with rituals around letting down and perusing what my psyche needs to thrive on. Every time I'm knocked off base, affected, or lost, my inner homing pigeon knows how to get back to inner zone. This homing pull is embedded in my psyche and comes with me everywhere. Accordingly, when I'm asked a question there might be a long pause; I might be asked if I am still there since I'm in deep silence. I am still there, but I've gone home to get something—that something being my answer.

The Good Witch has insulated herself; she's put a shield around herself and home that's impenetrable. The shield is impassable to negativity and dark vibrations, though there's a chimney-like opening at the top for when Bad Bitch goes off the deep end, so her chaotic energy can depart. Bad Bitch is

affected by the empathy for life that she feels all around her; her sadness for suffering is mixed with paranoia and she feels anxiety. Who wouldn't in this crazy period of the darkness coming into light? There's work to be done on the be calm, stay in the now, and be positive sector, because it takes commitment. Our mental state and how we move through these radically changing times will be key to our good outcome. We must hold ourselves above the fray for it's in solitude where our power stands and, when we come home to ourselves, we access it.

Our abode, the dwelling we escape to is the physical expression of our consciousness. Some of us are travelers and wanderers, so our homes are in our backpacks, while others have a garage full of saved inheritances that need to be dealt with. When we hoard old stuff for *just in case*, we do not trust that what's needed in the future will be perfectly delivered. Homes are living energy fields meant to nurture their inhabitants. The way we honor where we live represents all the ways the Universe honors us. So, as we clear space, give things away, organize and clean, we are treating our home and what we own as holy. We're setting the stage here for the way we live on the planet, our greater home. Our rituals and ceremonies honor where and how we exist and hold us as ceremoniously as we hold ourselves.

Humans are nesters, we like to lodge in spaces that reflect our inner joy back to us. Our homes are a living palette of the changing paradigm of who we are in the reflection of our dreams. While our dreams change, our needs change, so we

have to define what is now viable, what is necessary and what no longer supports us. I constantly move the furniture and go through closets and drawers, compiling things to give away. I have come to a place in spirit where I want less; I want fewer choices, no clutter and less responsibility. I once needed a lot of stuff, outfits for just in case. It was because I wasn't sure who I was and had to try on personas. Even going to meet real estate clients, my goal was to capture them, so my style would imitate who I thought they were. While they flung their Prada bag into the back seat of my car, I flung mine right next to theirs. Now I'm honoring who I really am and being different, because I've come home to myself.

During the time when we lived in upstate New York at the meditation ashram, I had a strong nesting instinct and would turn our one room into a haven. Every time I got our space to the place where it felt like a safe escape, there would be a knock on the door, and I was told I had to move. After the fifth time I gave up and decided that I would escape into meditation instead. Once again asked to move, I was escorted to new living quarters to find a large renovated suite overlooking a quiet garden. I did not move again until I left with practically nothing but a solidified stance on a cosmic way of being. The lesson wasn't about not getting what I wanted; it was about receiving what I needed in order to anchor into a higher state. Once I got there, I received what I wanted, being a sanctuary to live in that reflected my peaceful essence.

Spaces have history and personality and they hold a resonance of all the people who've lived there prior or have even built the place. A friend, house shopping in upstate New York, was about to sign a contract when her empath daughter arrived; she sat quietly on the steps and had a chat with the house. After a few minutes she told her mother, "You can't buy this house; it gets bored when there is not a lot of activity going on. It doesn't like solitude and will disturb you if you don't comply with its energy field." My friend, not the dinner-party-throwing type or one with a house full of guests, agreed and moved on to look for a more tranquil abode. Another friend lives in a five-story brownstone where all the tenants are young and in party mode; they're excited about living in the city and want to connect with its energy. This friend is also young, but more of a recluse as he works at home. His building is good for him as it stimulates movement; he's the type who will stay in places forever and this building is pushing him to move.

As a realtor, I know that residences choose their tenants. A house can sit on the market for eons until the right buyer shows up. I always sit in ceremony with my listings and ask them what they need, so my friend's daughter knowing what that upstate house needed didn't surprise me. We can communicate with the energy in houses and ask it to change for us, because if we show a house love, it will love us back and give us what we want. It's all about respect for what exists and when we sit with respect within a space, we are partners in tandem. I have known buyers to move into

homes where everything is constantly going wrong. I know it's because they're not being sensitive to the house: cutting down too many trees, bulldozing the land and doing construction without consideration or love. I sold a home to a buyer who wanted to yank out all the bird's nests in the eaves; they had baby birds in them. I told him to live with them and carefully move them once the babies have flown, or else he would be disturbing nature. I warned him that he could have a flood if he didn't listen, as nature would disturb him in return. He looked at me like I was crazy—and then listened, because he believed me.

Houses and buildings have karma. All dwellings have stories, even newly built ones. I once represented a new construction where the lower level had some very dark energy. It was finished as a screening room with an extra family room in a very luxurious style, but I got chills every time I went down there. When I tried to clear the space, it wouldn't let me, then weeks later, the owner suddenly passed away. It was one of the few houses I couldn't sell, because the house didn't like me. Then again, I've sold many houses that other brokers couldn't sell, because probably the house didn't like them either. It's all in the relationship we have with the abode in question. I now know it's not my job to fix and clear everything. Some places are not part of my business, like an aisle in my local health food store that I purposely don't walk down, as there is something dark and weird going on there. As an empath, I feel spaces as clearly as I feel people's fears and grief, and I'm often not invited to fix

these things, it's just best to leave love and light there to do what it can.

It's a fact that space is alive and interacts with our energy field. Spaces hold us, though sometimes they demand attention and we have to take care of them. Other times they push on us to move and change our reality; the neighbor's loud television, the child who's constantly running and jumping above us until midnight . . . it's the Universe getting in on moving us out. Spaces have energy vortexes, sometimes they capture us until we transform ourselves and are then released. I inherited my mother's apartment in the building where I grew up in Manhattan; it was not a necessary shelter, but a pied-à-terre I kept for pleasure. I felt the soul of my mother in this apartment and slept like a baby there.

There were times I didn't go there for months and it was crazy to keep this apartment, but I savored her energy. I'd emptied it out and made it mine, yet my maternal connection was still immersed in this space. This apartment is a haven for me, it reminds me of what shines in my spirit—which is crazy, because New York City is intense, and it demands a lot to stay in balance. When I go to this apartment, I'm nurtured by a wave of love; other times, the apartment tells me it's okay to give it up as I'm ready to nurture myself in new ways. This apartment relationship is a process that is saying: *I will hold you for as long as you need.*

Good Witch knows when it's time to move, as her broom calls her to search for new places to thrive in. Bad Bitch needs constant healing space and visualizes the perfect

residence; it has pink bougainvillea climbing up a white wall on a quiet sunlit lane. My team is on the lookout to find this imaginary dwelling, this place that lives in my heart. My soul is working on manifesting it because I've charged it to do so. Meanwhile, I've been guided to make where I now live a sacred household.

Treating where we reside as our sanctum opens a way for us to stay in our element and still attract movement. It doesn't matter if we lodge in one place forever or become wanderers. It doesn't matter where we live, just how we live. We have to dream our way so, consider your consciousness as an interior decorator that goes shopping while you dream. We might be sitting around dreaming of bougainvillea climbing up white stucco walls, while our psyche is putting in cosmic orders for all the new vases we will need.

A friend had created the perfect place to live and is now constantly bombarded by noise. Looking to move and not finding another place he could afford, he decided to make this space that he loved, work. He might go to bed with earplugs listening to his breath; he might go away on weekends when street fairs are happening. Sometimes he gets totally lost in the music he is composing; this consignment is his form of ceremony. Getting comfortable in a place that is not comfortable teaches us how to insulate, while it pushes us to find a spot of magic in a shit pile. It's not to say that we should agree with being uncomfortable. We should never agree, though it's something we constantly dance with. When discomfort pushes us to leap off of it, especially when

there's nowhere else to go, it's telling us that it's time to create more of what comforts us around it.

Circumstances around our lack of control build up and we feel hopeless in extreme itchy sweater syndrome. I was often sent to school as a child in these kinds of sweaters and could not focus on anything other than taking it off. As a result, I was not all there, I was mostly in dreamland. Because of the extreme itchiness, I became a great escape artist, a skill I still have. I no longer wear itchy sweaters and when I'm uncomfortable I turn up the music and clean. If you come to my house and it's immaculate, I've been through a bout of discomfort. My scrubbing rituals go beyond good housekeeping; it's my soul that's cleansing my reactions. When I'm done, I've shifted huge mental energy and my house feels peaceful.

The vibration in our home reflects our mental state; sometimes things break, need rehab, demand attention. A friend confided that when she was a houseguest during a time she felt out of control, the houses she visited had mishaps, pipes broke and flooded, and mine was one of them. I didn't realize it was her fault, but she figured it out when she got home, and her dishwasher flooded. I thought about Carrie, the Firestarter, and was glad my friend wasn't angry, just emotionally flooded enough to break my toilet, the place where we dump our shit. Coincidentally, I had just bought a winter retreat in a building on a beach, where old timers who'd lived there had formed a clique and didn't like newcomers. I thought about all the kinds of people I didn't

like, mostly unconscious types (quite a large group), and realized I had to clear that impression. Our projections are what come to surround us in reality, so look around at what's breaking and falling apart, find its reflection inside yourself and clear it.

There's another world beyond our sense perceptions, and when we look for it, we receive images of it. Every happening in the world was once an unseen image that came to be, so in the ritual of exploring past reality, we peruse uplifting impressions that we hold our focus on until they spark. I love to see stories hidden in shadows, like the ones I saw as a child, when I traveled into images in wallpaper, reflections, and light beams. Staring into these things in an ethereal way, I'd go into altered states that led to mindless ceremonies that were imaginative and healing. I had no idea what was really going on, but if I'd had a bad day or experience, off I went and when I returned, I was in serene bliss.

In our healing zone we let our guard down; we go bra-less and embrace ourselves. Delving with courage into a labyrinth of wrong considerations, it takes overcoming ego to look at the reflections we've created that don't serve us. Once we face the monsters, instead of slaying them, we take wisdom from them. They will tell us the ugly tales we need to heal and teach us compassion. We come out of the labyrinth understanding there's no us-and-them, so we handhold our broken hearts and pick up the shattered pieces. Every time there's a disturbance we stop to address it and ask it for its message. We step into its zone—not in fear or anger, but with

steadiness to ask the most important question: What do we need to rearrange in this situation and what do we need to rearrange in ourselves to pass through it?

One morning during a writing session, someone on my street was using a leaf blower; they pollute the planet and are so buzzingly noisy. My first thought was to feel enraged at the stupidity of these machines and, suddenly I had traveled into the sound of it and was gone on some weird sci-fi trip my inner child was playing with. Within moments, I was feeling deep inner peace, even while the noise was still quite loud. I went into such a deep state of homing into myself that the outer world shifted, and I was in deep solitude in the midst of commotion. I made a note to remember this feeling and use it while in the outside world.

We're being pushed beyond ourselves and also being pushed to retrieve the magic we need. On shaky ground, we must meanwhile create harmony inside our being, the homeland. It's a process to find our way when the winds of change are blowing through, whilst at the same time, discretions invite us to peruse further prospects. I open the doors in my mind to air out the rooms, while I look around at other options, some of which blatantly say: ***Don't trespass here!*** Why? Because certain terrain is a waste of time if we are not ready to shift through it. We are the house within the house and what a mansion of unexplored wings we possess as we run down hallways and climb unknown back stairs. Suddenly, we bump smack into a burst of believability; it's handing us the keys to get our house in order.

We move through chaos by seeing its opportunity. In this lifetime, one of my most important relationships is with someone who I feel, many times, doesn't get me. I see this relationship as a great healing opportunity on lifetimes of not putting down wounds, to rise above them. While we hold great love for each other, we may never get to our clear homeland together. Though in the fact that I recognize the possibility as being enough, it's already happening in my heart because if I don't hold a sense of lack, it doesn't exist.

Lack is a state of mind we must use to impose a sense of freedom. Like not being imprisoned by responsibility or by being pushed to use a deficit to start anew. I know a person who in summer, lives in a most luxurious community by the sea, in his car. He showers at the gym and does actual business. He just likes this lifestyle of moving around. Being low on funds doesn't stop him, for whatever it takes can be a great story if we use it as one. He is a survivalist that holds beauty and bliss as a priority no matter what.

The Good Witch is at home on her broom, she's always elevating, while Bad Bitch is scrubbing the toilet and has now decided she's no longer in deep shit. It's not the story that matters most, it's the feeling we have in our stories and how we ritualize them. I put my good feelings on a shrine and prostrate to them, and it doesn't matter if they make sense because they don't. What matters is that I pay homage to them, so they grow.

As a realtor, homes are my passion. During open houses, I sit in other people's living rooms when they're not home

and the house tells me everything I need to know about who lives there. It tells me who is off-kilter and who needs love. Sometimes I move the furniture around or bring an item to leave there to shift the energy. I see houses as living beings, extensions of us. They give us a place to crash, to retreat, to heal, and when we treat them as sacred places, the energy builds up to support us. As we go out in the world, this energy comes with us, so home becomes wherever we go. It's like that saying: *Wherever you go, there you are.* Therefore, whatever we value is what values us. The keys to our castles are hidden in cherished realms where we write the stories. These stories are all our creations, as either we agreed to them on some level, or we made them up and hid our keys in them.

The keys are:

- See your living space as an extension of how you cherish your life. Even if you have little in the material world, honor your space as a treasure.
- Create an altar in your space and on this shrine place photos of your loved ones, your saints, dreams, prayers, and sacred objects. Light candles, burn incense, place flowers, and make other offerings here. Ask for what's sacred to be blessed, charged, and protected.
- Smudge your space daily, even mentally. This includes your body, your car, your laptop, your pets,

and anything you think of. You can even do this from a distance.

- Open all the windows, even in winter, to keep it fresh and enhance airflow.
- Get lost in the things you do to take care of yourself. Consider even taking out the garbage as an offering of being grateful for what you've used.
- Let go of things you're done with and give away as many things as possible.
- Lighten your junk load, clean your fridge, your drawers, your closets and organize things, because clogged, over-filled spaces represent your energy field.
- Have cleaning sessions where you change up the energy in your environment by exalting it to sparkling. This includes your workspace, your office, your car, even your yoga mat.
- Protect your space; sprinkle salt in a circle around your house or across the front door of your living space and windows. You can do this in your mind, if necessary.
- Always thank your shelter and when you leave it, surround it in blessings.
- Before sleep, mentally shield your home and yourself in a silver bubble filled with white light and command that only what is for your highest good may pass.
- When a new space is desired, honor where you now live and ask it to expand its horizons for you, then

ask it to help you find another place and to let you go.

- Spaces have energy fields that are alive, so work with them.
- Play music, keep plants, have pets, and love in your space.
- Have a meditation area, a healing room, or a mat where you sit in prayer.
- Say daily prayers and affirmations when you rise and before bed.
- Consider the bathroom as a sanctified cleansing room. Imagine that your shower or bath holds holy water and that all you do there is clear sludge and polish up your goodness.
- Cook wholesome meals that you share, as all you give will return to you a thousand-fold.
- Always clear the energy around you, take your shoes off at the front door, and as you wash your floors, imagine you are washing the hall of a temple.
- Treat your home as a sanctified space, so it will honor you as a cherished guest.
- Surround yourself with beautiful tales, as beauty is a direct source of divine energy.
- It doesn't matter where we live, really. It only matters how we live within ourselves.
- Bless everything you have as a gift from God.

Minding our Business . . .

We can be anyone, from the garbage pickup person to the CEO of a tech company, though the boon of our livelihood is when we're: *Dynamically Engaged.* If you don't feel charged about what calls you, the spark is in there and you need to find it. Even if the spark seems impossible, that's just an illusion, a detour that needs to be circumvented. New ideas call for promise, so when we question all the reasons why we're nuts and doing it wrong, know you're not crazy, nor are you doing it wrong. You're doing it, which is all that matters. The energy around our ideas have life force, thus dedication is the ritual that activates momentum. If there are delays while struggling through the current labyrinth towards your new means, know it's still happening—and keep going.

Bad Bitch was gyrating in the neither-here-nor-there zone; she was done with where she was but had not found her new way. She kept trying to go back to the old ways, trying to shove her foot into a shoe that no longer fit and this dynamic was beating her up. She finally got that she needed to sit in discomfort and wait it out, and then understood that her pregnant pause was about a state of being, not doing. How wacko that we now have to define our reasoning

for doing and not doing, and also be in tune with the appropriate moment for each of these endeavors. All parameters have rules, so being addicted to action won't cut it when serenity is the activity needed for the clearing of emotional hysteria. Once Bad Bitch surrendered into what the moment was calling for, her perspective shifted. She began to play with new impressions, which had directions she could follow–and becoming the Good Witch was one of them.

A friend, who is a diva homemaker and chef, had a television show and published many books on her arts-and-craft style ideas. She purchased four homes with me that she fluffed and flipped for great profits. These refurbished homes were all unique and we literally fell in love with each of them. I'm not sure what happened but suddenly her contracts were up and not resigned; her investment money ran out, and it seemed she was suddenly in a boat with leaks. Not being in her normal flow put her in extreme discomfort and she spent much of her time in prayer.

I'm sure she was asking, begging, bartering for a break, as we all do when slammed to our knees. It was a long, two-year period of stress, but she never lost faith because she's a survivor. She even survived a drive-by shooting as a teenager, where she was shot in the leg. In her down time, always looking for the message in things and for what's sacred in everyday life, she wrote essays on her faith that she read in her church. It was there that a current publisher discovered her and signed her to a new book deal. Crazy good, how she

never expected her next role to go from homemaking to sharing about God, but there she was surfing a new wave with passion.

The charismatic energy we feel in our undertakings is our directive that moves the way it needs, and when we're aligned with its motion, it clears gridlock. Another friend constantly moved his furniture around as his energy was continually shifting and he needed to frequently realign with it. Sometimes the most mundane things must all coordinate prior to their lift-off. This is a time to do crosscheck; passion is the throttle that calls us to align with it and feel our way around.

Since our senses know way more than our thinking minds, we have to feel the way into our flow, but first we have to clear the way. We all have an intuitive vein that sometimes will get clogged with mental traffic and we question things instead of trusting ourselves. Meditation is the ability to witness our mind-flow without falling into it, while it empowers our higher connections. We sit, we watch, we breathe, we squirm, we continue to sit, and clear the cache so answers will come. Alas, until we get to our sage insight we wait and continue to move the furniture around.

The Tibetan Buddhist Saint Milarepa was a black magician and a murderer until he met his master Marpa. Marpa instructed Milarepa in the labor of building a tower, though every time he finished it, he was told to take it down and rebuild it. This reassembling and destroying of the tower went on for decades and was such a severe austerity that

Milarepa grew so frustrated that he planned to take his life. Poignantly, right before ending it all, he was hit by a spark of Bodhi knowing and became enlightened. It wasn't about the perfect tower that represented a place of higher vision, it was about a continual restructuring in order to clear his way there. The point is that it took sweat equity for him to burn his karma and live as a liberated realized yogi.

During the times when my friend was moving the furniture, I thought he was like Milarepa who had no idea why he kept doing the same task over and over. I pondered if my friend was in a similar act of purification and that his task was not to question it, but to show up to do what was needed. It was about total dedication to what was necessary to evolve. Learning about Milarepa, I took away that it doesn't matter what our task is; it matters what our devotion is and how it manifests great outcomes. Until that devotion comes to a head we're still preparing. The *Bingo* premise is to understand that when our doing becomes venerable, things suddenly shift into gear, the throttle clicks in and turns on, our destiny comes into focus—and off we go.

I have an accountant I believe is a secret saint who wants to help his clients do better in life. Though he's quite wealthy, being a money-positive person, his clientele is across the board financially. I referred him to a friend who'd mentioned they considered money fearful and withholding. My friend, after conversing with this accountant is now holding the perspective that money is their new best friend and not an enemy that would beat them up. Working in real

estate, there were some deals that left me feeling battered and psychically bleeding when I went to collect my check. People are always trying to cut the deal and often what they're really cutting is the appreciation and the respect for the value of another human being. Such miserly values bring an ungenerous quality of life.

Coming across the generous of heart is a sign that we're in alignment with this similar kind of grandiosity. Working on a real estate deal where the buyers were ruthless, I asked my architect that I always hire to help, if I was cursed and why was it always these kinds of miserly people at the table? He said. "No, you are blessed, totally blessed, and I love you." I don't even really know this man, but what he said moved me and felt true. The message came through a stranger, that architect, saying I was cherished. It meant that no matter what rotten fruit was in the basket, the one good piece is what matters. Behind the scenes, some of us are really secret saints—my architect and accountant are both ones.

A new manager in my real estate office made me a better person. He never once told me what to do or should-ed me, it was just his presence. When I was in his company, I wanted to show up as the best version of myself. Being around people who hold themselves well is attractively magnetic. In business, we come across all types and we have to deal with them. I used to do battle with the threatening reputation of: *Oh no, here she comes!* It's now, someone call Lori (my professional name) to get this job done. Being more

patient, I stand back and wait for what needs to happen to show itself.

I rented a home to the loveliest family, though when I asked the landlord to sign a document that would cover me as their broker (in case they ended up purchasing the house), he went off on a tangent about how he didn't have to sign it and didn't owe me anything. We stood in his yard and he looked like a devil with smoke coming out of his ears, going off on a diatribe that made no sense. In the past, I would have let him have it but this time I just stood there and let him rant until he was done. I was watching him in amazement as he went forth into his story of being screwed and what he would and wouldn't do. Finally, he stopped his tirade and I said, "Please sign the paper and we can negotiate the terms if it happens." He said, Fine. I find that if someone is blowing off hot air, it's best to let them, don't touch it, and come back after.

A good business model is one that benefits the whole; it includes all the players and becomes like the arms of a dancing Shiva. Each arm has its own reasoning that works for the best outcome. In real estate, there's an *only-what's-best-for-me* motif running. Everyone wants to win, and it has come to the point where greed has destroyed the playing field. Then again, there's always a way to hold one's own in any game, it's by staying elegant and above the mire. A tenant was haggling over a rental fee when the energy contracted. Meanwhile, the landlord was so elegant that his energy overrode my tenant's penny-pinching behavior and he sealed

the deal with his charms. We naturally hook into the best possibility when our energy is held higher than the lower energy running.

It's interesting, even as an experiment, to hold our own when others are not on our same vibration. I recently donated a large pile of just-read books to my local used bookshop. They were expensive books. On the way out I picked up an old beat-up Wild West paperback for my husband. Surprisingly, the bookseller overcharged me for it. I left, and told my husband, who said, "Some people will jump over a dollar to pick up a penny." I felt the woman should have given me the used, very beat-up book, or it should have been a quarter instead of three dollars, but her desperateness for the extra money did not stop me from continuing to gift my books to her store. The point is that we have to stay in our source, even while others don't.

Stepping into the attributes of high energy fields and what they have to offer, the act of a ritual will attract good outcomes. I've buried many Saint Joseph statues (the patron Saint of realtors) at houses I've listed to sell. On my knees in the dirt, digging up rocks, talking to a plastic statue, telling it my desires and asking it for blessings is about investing energy in magical beliefs. One house did not sell for three years, the sellers wouldn't listen. My little Saint Joseph statue just hung out there and I'd forgotten about him. Finally, I was about to lose the listing when I remembered I'd buried the statue and had to go dig him up. First, I had a new conversation with Saint Joseph, asking one more time for his

blessings in selling the house. In a week, the house went into contract with my own buyer, who came out of nowhere. This development led me to invest even more energy into my magical beliefs.

Against all odds is a great energy field where we empower the thought that what we need to happen will happen, even in ways we don't expect. I've found that when I invest in what goes against the common grain, my conviction multiplies whatever I throw into its vortex. Others moan when they've bought into the energy field of less in a down market, while I play the exempt card and downplay what's going on. I put on blinders and keep going, though since passion is my ride sometimes it goes into donkey mode and refuses to move—that's when I know I'm changing direction. We don't always know where we're going and then suddenly take a strange turn because passion needs to explore the unknown. It will try on ideas that change our direction and we must follow it, even when we have no idea of the outcome.

Sitting in my new apartment overlooking the ocean in Florida during a storm, the palm trees are bending in the wind, the ocean's churning and I have no idea what we are doing here. I keep asking my husband and he keeps replying that we're healing. I am sick of healing from *God knows what* and want to be immersed in my next passion play. This timeout is an amazing reprieve where I am working on this book. This is my passion play. It's not about success or the outcome; it's about the time and space to do something my heart needs to do. It's not really understandable to me as

Bad Bitch is often a control freak and worried about money, while Good Witch keeps whispering there is treasure in this moment. Okay, I get the message that my new business is about calming down and loving where I am—and it will go off from there.

Meanwhile, there's chaos in the world, the weather, a state of emergency, an insane virus, and I'm sitting here looking for treasure in this moment. Am I crazy? Yes, I am a fearful, fearless, cautious wild spirit finding my way in the unknown. Uncertainty is up for exploration, but we can't figure it out by Googling it, although an astrology reading might help. We might spend hours easing ambiguity (the voice from Hell) while calming ourselves down by accepting that practicing mindfulness in action is what's up right now. Maybe we're not always in auto-positive mode and we have to work on it. It's with constant awareness to know what we need to lift off of especially when we're in a discomfort zone, a disappointment zone, and a this is not good enough zone. During the times when we don't know what's going on, we are clearly being shown what's not going on and the trick is: We don't invest in what bothers us and just give it room to move out.

Knowing the next move requires patience and skill. We might have to wait it out and use the time to collect information and plan a mode of operation. Meanwhile zest is collecting ingredients for our new manifestations, while we're minding the energy field around a calling. Meanwhile the outside world is banging on the door, demanding money

for bills, and we have to do a money run. I always think of it as having an affair. I'm madly in love and so if I have to go sell houses, my secret affair is still carrying me when things become annoying. Writing is my treasured rendezvous that inspires me, I still have to support myself and not cut corners to stay in its arms, so I show up to my job, but since I'm deliriously in love, this passion bleeds into the *all I have to do* zone and no area of my work is minimized.

The Good Witch, my invisible friend, says: Timing is about our practical magic that tells us what it needs for us to perform it. It also says when to fling everything else to the wayside. Considering that everything we do has a spirit, when I went to yoga it told me: *You Need This*. After a while, it told me to go walk in nature and dream, you can come back later. My writing has a spirit that I can't live without that says: *Do whatever it takes to make time to come back to me.* Real estate also has a spirit that says: *Even when you hate me, you will always love me, so keep the door open.*

Being in conversation with the spirit of things we find the magic that's instilled in them. It's not so much about the activity around our passion as it is about tapping into the source of it. Once linked in, our passion reveals directives that enhance everything around it. A directive I got when I published my last book, after a copywriter told me not to publish too many because they will sit in boxes and collect dust in my attic, was to ignore her. I sold out the boxes of books, ordered more, and sold them out too. The book told me what it needed me to do and I heard it. My first

published book told me it might not sell well at first, but that after I had honed my skills, it would sell out later. I wondered if that meant after I died. The book then laughed at me and asked, *"Does it really matter?"* It didn't.

True surrender is when we're called to do something and so we do it and then it's out of our hands. Once again, our power place is not always in the outcome but in the way that we go. As when we're walking in our power, we feel it even when we're going sideways. Though if suddenly, we realize that we're not in our power place, it means our viewpoint is off. The barometer reads: disoriented. It's because we have misplaced the magical perception of knowing there's something to be had in this moment and instead of finding it, we went emotionally out there, losing our awareness. So, as we pull the mundane through the eye of a needle, we're transforming ourselves, expanding our life-force and making offerings. Plans get thrown to the wayside when the Good Witch is traveling the course of action that shows me what to do as we go. Since all things must change to grow, an important aspect of *Minding Our Business* is knowing that when nothing is going on—we're germinating and what's growing is a gift from God.

Minding our Business Rituals:

- Believe in yourself and stay soulfully connected—this is a mandatory first step in defining your special vocation and livelihood.

- Be devoted to your endeavor even when the journey goes into a labyrinth and you have to go a bunch of wrong ways to find the right way.
- Our souls are the directors of operations that define our craft; hear them.
- Speak highly of your undertaking to juju more magic into it.
- Dismiss all limited concepts and never invest your beliefs in the otherwise.
- Understand the karma of your struggles.
- When struggling, you're in the process of clearing blockages and opening doors.
- Mentally talk to your business, tell it what you need, write it notes, make offerings.
- Practice being one-pointed, even in unknowingness.
- Solidify commitments and if you've made them, finish them, as promises deliver.
- Don't get lost in time frames or the thought that things are taking too long, just believe in the fact that it's happening.
- Understanding timing is about believing in perfect sequence and that you're exempt from common chronology and time frames.
- Invoke passion into your business, invoke vision, invoke new ideas.
- Offer what you're doing for the good of humanity. You might wonder if humanity needs this exact

stint—offer it anyway. Even if one person gets it and needs it—it's worth it.

- Include blessings—bless every interaction as a gift, including the hard ones.
- Stay in conversation with the spirit of things and look for signs.
- Ask your ideas what they need to grow and do all you can to support them.
- Envision your business growing, and constantly thank it for doing so.
- Bask in the feeling of success, even if you're in the beginning stages.
- Trust new energy; acknowledge the flow.
- Trust your passion and even if the payoff hasn't arrived, keep trusting it.
- Place reminder notes around claiming your prosperity.
- Every time you receive money, thank the universe and give some away to help others.
- Always pick up pennies; the universe is letting you know your abundance is arriving.
- Help others along the way.
- The way in which we treat others is how we will be treated.
- Consider yourself in the flow even when nothing's happening.
- Understand that since we're in perpetual creation, even the ebb is part of the flow.

- Make amends for your shortcomings; it's not about winning, but fair play.
- Think profitably.
- Profit grows in the vision of its actualization and the bliss felt while creating it.
- When pulled out of your game or when the game changes, know that you're being called to recalibrate your motives and moves.
- Be a good loser! Losing only means as much as we make it to mean.
- We all have up and down seasons; it's part of the movement. Don't judge these intervals, honor what they're saying and use them to motivate your next move.
- Things may change drastically—it means we too have to change drastically.
- If someone else makes the deal, gets the promotion, writes a bestseller, wins the lottery, be happy and celebrate windfalls to access a good fortune party.
- Strokes of luck come out of left field when least expected and staying in awe attracts them.
- Ritually light white candles for light-filled energy, green candles for prosperity, red ones for love, pink for peace, yellow for happiness, blue for protection, orange to wake something up, and purple to instill magic. Write your affirmations on them to signal the universe to participate.

- Acknowledge that you're always in training, so whatever's happening, find the teaching.
- Keep waving your wand and stay in your magical lane.

Our Kindred Ties . . .

Our relatives and past ancestors are a soul group of companions, all playing out different roles in different lifetimes to support each other's awakenings on this planet. You must agree, it's kind of insane to think we've all arrived here as awakened beings only to go comatose around our greater existence and have forgotten who we are in the grand scheme of what is transcendent. We might think our relatives are these overbearing people who are annoyingly needy and try to control us—I did. The truth is our relatives and ancestors are not even close to whom they appear to be but are the soul group that we arrived in this lifetime to grow with. True that sometimes our relatives seem un-awakened and difficult, though maybe imagine them as actors leveraging us to re-awaken. The point is that when the relatives go crazy, they're still the tribe we're going to the heart of the matter with because their existence is relative to ours.

I once didn't speak to my mother for six months, or shall we say my bitch did not speak to her bitch. She didn't even call me on my birthday. Her bitch was supreme and trumped my bitch. I broke down first and called her, and immediately her bitch went down and she was my mother again. She had

dual personalities and when the mean one appeared it was scary. Granted, when I did not take her craziness personally, I could see her wounds and how her trespasses against me came from her own lack of self-love. She was such a gift to me in that her weaknesses gave me the strength to love myself beyond her dramas. We learn how not to be.

Most people act crazy when they need to express a truth they can't find. It's our dharma, a.k.a divine law to become sacred helpers assisting others to find and express their truth. *What do you need from me?* is a great question that stops the games and storylines. Even if there's no answer at least this question brings us an understanding of what we actually need. We might need to define our commitments, create a boundary or end a relationship. Going over what's been said or done doesn't matter as much as what our intention now is. Our highest motivation will always come back to love, so our discernment is the objective that overrides games and power struggles, bringing us to higher realizations.

A friend sent her ex-husband an angry letter accusing him of manipulating her emotionally. The letter nailed some personal points and when her ex-husband received it, he felt exposed and ashamed, so he acrimoniously cut off communication with her. This was not the outcome she intended. What she really wanted was for him to own his actions and be compassionate to her feelings. She got the opposite, now there wasn't any room for healing because he'd slammed the door. In lieu of this, my friend was continually sending him love but he was too wounded and staidly unforgiving.

The point is for us to own our wounds, resolve them with inner care and then acknowledge that unresolved emotional aspects create the exact karma we don't want because the pain will continue until we heal our side. My friend was sorry she sent the letter, but she healed her position by having compassion for herself and her ex-husband while continuing to wish him well. The animosity no longer existed on her side. In the end, her ex-husband came around to a place of peace with her because there was nothing other than that to hold on to.

I come from a long line of opinionated hate-mongers; my parents were social climbers who were always falling off their mountain. My mother constantly notified me about who we weren't talking to weekly. While immersed in an us-against-them modality, she would charm people into doing what she wanted by pretending she was their best friend, while she held the knife behind their backs. I inherited this genetic trait by holding onto accusations with a huge chip on my shoulder. My middle finger was frozen upright on both hands and, I was scary.

We inherit subliminal traits from our parents while some of us literally become them. When I tried on my mother's disposition, I had an experience of compassion for her fears, her confusion, and strengths—I felt all of it. At some point, we must use these heirloom identities as the compass to grow out of our parents' shadow and come into ourselves. To cut the cords on all the imposed behaviors we adopted from our parents grants us the ability live free from their restraints

while still having good will around them, and this is how we become our own saviors.

My mother and father loved to hate each other and then make up, and this pattern slayed my mother. She became depressed and literally stayed in bed for two years, smoking and drinking. One day she got up, put her cherished mink coat on over her disheveled pink nightgown and went out to walk the dog. She did this nightly in the early evenings and, one night she never came back. She'd gone missing! When found, after thinking she had jumped into the East River by our apartment to end it, I thought of her as a hero. She was so unhappy, and she did something about it, she left. She'd met another man who lived on the other side of the building while walking the dog. They'd been walking their dogs together for a week and one evening she went home with him and her story changed. My mother had the courage to leave my father, though in the end they celebrated what they originally loved in each other and even went to each other's weddings.

Since my parents both remarried, I inherited new relatives. My stepfather was a dream come true, while I nicknamed my stepmother, "Evil One." When my dad passed, my stepmother fled with his life insurance money, not listening to his last wishes to give my brother and me a share. We were young and both broke, but in the end, this pissed us off so much that we became highly successful in retaliation. We didn't speak to this woman for over two decades and were fine to go to our graves totally forgetting

she ever existed but exist she did. After many years holding a grudge against her, I was contacted by my stepmother on social media; it was the right time and I fell in love with her immediately. She was now in her eighties and I instantly felt like, so what if she took the money, she needed it more than we did. She never really was an evil one, I just saw her that way, and was able to love this woman unconditionally before it was too late.

The point is that our inherited gifts are to be found where we least expect them; they're hidden in the annoyances, the disgust, the betrayals, the hate and rage we feel. A son slams out of his family's home in the middle of a holiday visit, calling an Uber to drive him hours back to the city where he lives. His parents did nothing to instigate this; it was just the way they were that incited their son. He screamed, "I've had it with both of you," on the way out the door at one in the morning. It was an explosion that broke open his mind to realize that he was more enraged at his own lack of compassion than at his actual parents. The next day he apologized, because the healing he received from his realization was powerful. He'd broken a pattern, taught himself how to communicate and immersed himself in guilt-free love for himself and his parents.

The turnaround happens when we hold the desired outcome in our relationships as the objective and don't get lost along the way in the *craziness.* How do we do it? We don't back away and we don't beat ourselves up for our reactions. Instead we introspect, even scrutinize for the long-

term benefit we desire. By exploring our truth, we'll see where we broke our soul connections to loved ones, because our liberation exists in healing these contracts.

Prior to coming here, our contracts were about our ability to love beyond our wounded emotional aspects. My inner bitch always shrieks, "I'm done!" when stuck in an emotive tangent with a certain family member. My Good Witch reminds her she is far from done and must dive into doing what is called for to get back to love. Since love is a pattern breaker that goes where it needs to release us from ego prison, we might have to eat our own mental crow to then be gifted with a blessed dessert called reconciliation.

Someone has to go first in order to break familiar patterns that cause conflict. In doing so, we're breaking the historic chain for our legacy. For instance, there was a pattern of animosity among my family members that they would go to their graves with. When they got mad, huge drama ensued until one party was slayed and then the other would go in to save them. It was nuts. I tried this dynamic on my little brother when we were children; I took him to the park by our apartment, pushed him in the swing and then told him I was leaving him there alone. He was three, I was six. When he started crying, I ran back and saved him. I felt so needed, it was amazing. But why two children went to the park alone in New York City is a whole other dysfunctional story of parents not being all there.

I have to acknowledge that there was grace around my brother and I as children, in the fact that we survived our

parent's insanity. There was even more grace in the fact that we broke their patterns. Still, it was an energetic that many times sneaked back in to be dealt with over and over. I finally once and for all addressed that one schism and removed it as an implant. It was the loss of my niece that drew the line to show what's more important than being right, being needy, and having an inflated ego, as coming back to love matters more. Now, animosity in my family detours us back to love immediately because we have a rule: never to go to sleep angry.

It's important to know that the patterns will sneak back in through new relationships with people who will subliminally play out historic dramas with us, until we wake up and heal them. A past manager I worked with would have temper tantrums in the office; always yelling and portraying dramas of an ego nature. He reminded me of my father, and since I still had a wound about my father's behavior, this other man's drama hooked into that old wound. I took his childish display personally, until one day, while he was having one of his fits, I noticed that he was acting like a dog pissing on a fire hydrant to make his mark, all because he felt less-than. He looked so silly, but I also noticed his display was not personal and suddenly there was no hook there for me anymore.

When we heal a wound, there is swelling; it hurts, and we let it. It then reveals what it needs from us to heal. In my case it was understanding and compassion for my father who never learned how to communicate with women as his

mother was always traveling the world. In order to get her attention, he'd have to make a commotion. As far as the immature man in my office goes, I clearly defined the word *No!* I then drew a line that he could no longer even get near and he apologized.

We all want happiness and the way to have it is to put down all that's not it. When we indulge in things that make us happy, happiness becomes an offering. It's our dharma; the cosmic law of right action to be in heart spirit with our relations. Some of us may have gotten washouts on loving parents, while others have been blessed to be immersed in loving them. Either way, the dharma is about coming to the realization of perfection around our relations and finding a way to come into a healing with them—no matter what. As we eliminate our ignorance, we eliminate our suffering. The only way to come to inner peace is by training ourselves to keep returning to its natural abode. If we don't, then no matter how many good wishes we campaign for, we will not experience happiness.

My mother, after her new husband passed on, fell back into depression and her old ways of manipulating love. She was hard to be around, but I showed up with boundaries and was her good daughter till the end. She pushed on those boundaries to break them, though it was the love I had for myself that held them in place. I considered her my greatest teacher since I taught myself to honor her nasty assets; the ones that brought out the worst in me, so I could transform them in myself.

When I made peace with my own nasty bitch, my mother's even meaner bitch calmed down so there was no one left for her to fight with. The depths of my mother's suffering forced me to come into mindfulness and higher understanding around what she was going through and trapped in. Captured by her pain, she acted out, and when I no longer took her attacks personally, I became a role model for her. In many ways we're all role models for each other, though at times when we're ambushed, emotions and circumstances are hard to get beyond. Each time we liberate ourselves from these tangents, we show ourselves and others what's possible.

Many friends have sacrificed for their families because their concept of loyalty is their way of showing love. My dharma is to love myself enough to be able to offer it. Our relations have an intrinsic nature, so coming into love by any way possible is mastery. A family legacy that holds anger and lacks forgiveness is simply about us doing our dharma to change that. I come from a long line of quarrelsome women, even my grandmothers hated each other. My mother and her favorite sister were always fighting, though the newer generation being my cousins and I, cleared and healed this legacy by genuinely loving each other. One cousin even gave another a needed kidney, as the throwback of animosity from our ancestors was not passed down, it was harmonized. It doesn't matter what the story is or ever was–the dharma of a story is about what we do with it now.

Our dharma changes in different situations, so how we

align with it is to go to the bigger picture and look at where the paths lead. I once needed to be successful to know if success had real power, thereafter I needed to be considerate when I wasn't. Each hurdle we eclipse leads to another level of being. Exploring cosmic wisdom, the dharma is to be a seeker, and in finding our wisdom, the dharma is to share it. Some people have the dharma to *Just Get Real.* That's a hard one, where we go into our own dressing room and take off everything that doesn't fit and leave it there. Every time I have to do this, I expand energetically as the cleared energy draws me back to who I am in spirit. My sacred self is a whole other being, free of encumbrances, impatience, anger, and fear. Imagine living in this state–it's enlightened.

Our experiences always revolve around relationships that are rated by how well our exchanges go, such as forgiving someone because we understand that being human is a feat of trial and error. Love is the acceptance of all aspects of our humanness; it's an open space where the difficulties around how we relate shift us. A co-worker in my office accused me of something that never happened. She believed, after her customer contacted me directly to ask a question, that I was trying to steal him. This made me think about how often I react to paranoia; we think others are doing things and maybe they are, but our reaction is our decree and staying out of it is a power place. I tried to explain that her customer and I knew each other prior and that I considered him her buyer now, but she was too into having a discrepancy with me. I let it go and she held onto it.

We are all hanging out in the worlds we create from our expectations, living out the magnetic attraction created from these beliefs. In an affinity with the highest forms of kinship we treat others as family, because on some level we're all a ménage of relatives once removed. Consider that we're everything: a potpourri of all aspects merged into one being. When we're challenged, we're edgy, bitchy, and dangerous. When we're serene, we're mighty, loving, compassionate beings, though the question is can we embrace all of ourselves? We must, as it's the only way to heal.

I have embraced my Bad Bitch with compassion, for she's not afraid to speak out. She's a powerhouse who's now learned communication skills beyond her array of fierce curse words. She guards the questionable side of me; the side that gets lost when at times I don't know who I am, as I change like a chameleon. She calls me back when I've gone too far and is actually (I repeat) the one who went to the tower and retrieved the Good Witch to pave our way. Playing many parts in my saga, my Bad Bitch doesn't need approval and has taught me that wanting recognition is a sign that I'm not fully endowed in my own passion. She is also the one who, when I go to the mirror, says: "Screw being the fairest of them all, be a lightning bolt of magic! "

The relationship we have with all aspects of ourselves is a panoramic view of how we relate, period. In the embrace of ourselves with the intention to balance all oppositions, we enhance the bigger picture. The game is to look at your stories, see where the turbulence is, what causes reactive

emotions, what is repetitive, and know these are the gifts we get to grow through. Therefore, audaciously use everything to transcend what does not hold faith. Even when you slip, get back up and always walk in the highest way as a kindred tie with all that exists, for this is how we elevate our world!

Relationship Dharma:

- Consider your relatives and ancestors as beings who play a role in your evolution.
- Our relations hold supreme gifts that we only receive when consciously elevated.
- Regard your relations as teachers; this includes your most difficult kinships.
- Everyone in our life is there for a reason, either as a healer, or one in need of healing.
- Make peace with your descendants, and if you can't do it in person, do it in spirit.
- Our spiritual considerations are powerful and considering another's well-being is an offering.
- In a disagreement, form follows thought; to shift the energy we must think well.
- When the relatives go crazy, look for their attributes and ignore their mood swings, which is the psyche trying to right itself.
- Our ancestors want what's best for us, even if they've never shown it. Once in spirit, they're

compassionately generous, desiring to give us what they couldn't provide prior.

- Send healing to all your descendants, siblings, and other kinfolk, knowing that you've all shared the gallantry to be born during this wild time of transformation.
- It takes valor to honor the courage in another person beyond what they're lost in.
- We're all here working it out and we need to work it out with each other.
- If there is a soul connection and we can't work out our differences in this lifetime, we will do it in the next lifetime, or when we meet in heaven.
- This lifetime is not for the fainthearted. It took great faith to come here, and it will take great courage to live well.
- Every time there's a rift in relations, sit in ceremony and do a healing to clear the energy and bring forth the goodness, even if it's just in yourself.
- Honor the relationships, even if they can't be healed on this plane.
- It's more about holding the intention of peace and love in the moment than visualizing the outcome. When we hold the intention strong, the outcome can slide right in.
- Things don't necessarily conclude in one lifetime, but are the gifts left over for newer generations of our clan to experience.

- In the now, it's fearless love that swats away all that's not part of our highest relations.
- Our past relatives are still around shining love and light on us.
- Our connections to our loved ones in the hereafter remain for eternity—till we meet again.
- The most holy state is to consider everyone a relative and know that the collective is also part of our kindred spirit.
- Consider there to be no difference in creed, color, or gender, and honor the heart and spirit of all beings, even when they're acting insane and you can't be around them.
- There are no real rules stating that we have to be a certain way, because when we accept ourselves, it becomes easier to allow radical differences.
- To honor and hold love with others means that we don't have to go along with their bylines, as holding love is more than enough.
- Remember that we're all playing roles and that we can change our role at any time.
- Ask for forgiveness, forgive yourself, and always do what brings peace.
- Send blessings to the relatives and ancestors, as all that we offer is what returns.
- The bigger picture will always require forgiveness, for we evolve in amnesty.

- When forgiveness is too hard, imagine how it will feel, and see yourself granting it anyway.
- Visualize your pardon affecting and softening the hardness that surrounds your heart.
- Play with compassion, sit with it, and let it soften all barriers.
- Our absolution is a reprieve from vindication.
- Mercy is aligned with the supreme compassion we have for ourselves as humans who are pulling out of battlefields and healing from wars.
- In the higher dimension we're at the gates of heaven slapping our relatives five for the great performances that have escalated our spiritual growth.
- In the end, our ancestors will welcome us, as we always come home to love.

Dream Weaver . . .

It was the start of my real estate career and I would visit the most expensive open houses on the market to see and feel the beauty of them. One house was an estate called Oz. It was on twenty acres with panoramic vistas and magnificent interiors. I remember running my hand over the bamboo wallpaper and receiving a vision that I would sell this house. It made no sense. I'd just started selling real estate and had not sold any houses of this caliber prior, though the message felt believable, so I stored it in my miracle-to-be file. Within a month I met a buyer driving by in a green convertible while I was standing on the road waiting for another customer who said he had a green convertible. I waved at this first gentleman thinking he was my customer. He pulled over and when I told him I was a realtor waiting for a certain buyer, he happened to tell me he was looking for a grand house. I took him to Oz, and he bought it. He then bought five other investment properties from me, as my vision had ignited a spark that manifested.

The ethereal impressions we receive are not passing fancies but are vibrating forces of energy that come to us as reveries with passports into reality. Though our pipe dreams

still have to pass through an immigration checkpoint of soul acceptance. This is where our soul customs officer steps forward and decides if we're ready to resonate with the new energy, while our heart official determines if our reverie being fulfilled will take us higher. Not all dreams pass into our promised land, especially the ego dreams of the Rolex with diamonds to prove that we're worthy of riches and can manifest them.

Granted, if we need to spend time exploring our worthiness, then yes, we might dedicate a decade or even a lifetime to material luxuries. It all depends upon our reasoning behind the dreams, though interestingly the higher our dream reasoning is the more material riches arrive that support our lifestyle in continuing to dream. When I originally fell in love with selling real estate, it was during a time when I did not own a home. I imagined redecorating and living in all the residences I visited for work because I was dreaming my home. Selling houses was easy because I was in love with the potential of them and would get lost in my dreams of making one mine. Shortly thereafter, I became successful enough to buy my own home and I bought one over my price range, thinking I would catch up and I did.

Once I had a home, my dream changed and I began delving into the magic, energy fields, and the escalation of dream possibilities, which then led me to write books about my experiences of these aspects. When we tap into the spark of a dream, it begins to weave itself into a creation and when

it's a soul destiny it manifests. Some of the dreams that come to us are huge, as they're for things way grander than we can understand at the time. These kinds of dreams are elevating us to catch up with them. When life takes a sudden turn, it's because we're going to the next level, and yes it feels quite weird though when we get there, we see it's perfect.

My brother is a commercial real estate developer who had a dream to build a ten-block-radius project that was like a small city in the arts district of Los Angeles. As soon as he finished this project, his life dramatically changed and none of what he'd done prior meant anything to him. It happened this way because he was being shown that manifesting his dream was one thing, but it was now more about what his life dream was in the bigger picture. He was being drawn to do healing work for other families who were going through the searing kind of loss he experienced after recently and unexpectedly losing his daughter to an overdose. With his experience as a developer, his prior completed building project was the turning point that gave him the financial freedom to focus on this life dream. The point is that our dreams are stepping-stones, and we might not know where they're going or what they will further accrue—we're just called to follow them.

Once a dream is manifested, we might think it's the tail end, but it's really a bridge to our next endeavor. We've all experienced everything from our greatest ecstasy to our worst nightmares in our dreams and visions, though not every experience needs to manifest in reality for it to be felt in our

bones and assimilated into our psyche. The Guru Neem Karoli Baba once declared that he was the richest man on Earth. Since he felt connected to all things, he believed he owned them. Once we feel this way, we own the actuality of things that don't even have to happen, because they're in our aptitude. I've been everything from queen of my world, a witch, a yogi, a top realtor, a writer of magical books, and a total bitch. So, since I've gone from being a real-estate rock star, to a humble aspirant, to the Good Witch and so much more, there have been so many personas to play with. Each persona has its own dreams and those dreams are avenues of creativity unfolding new destinies.

During a time when destiny took a turn, nothing I was doing seemed to be working. I had lost my mojo. It was a time demanding great faith for me to get through it with wisdom. There were days of huge angst when even my dreams went void. The test was one of supreme strength around holding onto ideas that had not even come close to manifesting yet. Constant messages were saying that even though nothing was happening, I was still on the right track. There was no escape, I could not go back to my old ways of doing things and there was no choice except to hang on. My saintly accountant told me to follow my dream, as I could afford to. I feared that if I stepped off the base of my business it would slip away and then I realized: "*Hey, I can always get it back later, if I want it.*" Every time I checked into my dream even when I was too exhausted to do anything about it, it excited me. My dream was still sparking though

the message was *just chill out*.

Chilling out is so not me. I am a do-er and my call to duty at this time was to do nothing and let the dream happen. The Universe was in on it, so even while I was gyrating, I had to accept that I was in right timing, to continue believing in my dream, and this had to be enough. Maybe it was a test of faith with emotional torture, to see if I had what it takes to follow through. When we get to the place of having no other choice, we have to surrender and wait for an opening. Eventually the energy began to move, so if you're reading this book, know you're holding a dream that has manifested. Dreams take time, they need space, and a period to just dream themselves. Here we align with what's important, drop the mundane life, roll up our sleeves and follow the dream.

We all have preordained soul excursions that we came here to be part of and being that we're geared to follow our aspiration, it's about having the courage to show up with authenticity. When the dream channel is open, all that's happening or what appears to be, doesn't matter. We might have to go the opposite way we think; we might have to take chances and stand around empty while we wonder if we're crazy. We might even have to shout into a bullhorn and yell about all the wrongs we witness. At times like this we will not be silenced because authenticity demands attention and is never complacent and takes a stand. We can be standing alone, figuring out what the pull is and the thing to acknowledge is that there is a pull. We're either being pulled

in deeper, pulled away, or pulled towards something new. It's like going into a riptide when the water looks calm and we're suddenly dragged out and end up sideways far from our blanket and when we get out of the riptide, we are not the same. When a dream grabs us, sudden changes are in alignment so we must fathom the underlying pull and get into a position to go with our hearts or be dragged.

Signs will flash, that's the pull. Recently I was keeping a desk in a real estate office, though I mostly worked at home. Another broker who curses like a truck driver and had it out for me, was assigned the desk next to mine. This was a sign to give up my desk. I realized it was no longer necessary to be in one place. I am not an office person anyway and how I got lost in being one is amusing. It goes to show how we get captivated by identities, and when it's time to drop them we get a sign. If we don't pay attention to that sign, we get a bigger one. If we still don't pay attention, we will get knocked off our stools. I laughed at the Universe for being hilarious by sending me a sign with an impression of my past tense, nasty bitch reflection.

Sometimes signs can be deceptive, tricky, and appear as anagrams. Mind you, I am many times anti-social, but I was subconsciously told to go look for opportunities. Invited to a summer party, we arrived to a group of very drunk people at the end of the driveway. We tried to sneak off, however we were seen. I wondered what the opportunity was and realized that my sign was showing me what it wasn't. I went to that party with my hand out for opportunities as I was in the

process of working on a dream. Instead I got an awareness that opportunity comes to us when we don't go looking for it. This could be argued, but I'm talking about the real thing. I'm talking about the Godsend opportunity; the one that goes beyond networking, like when the cosmos delivers a boon that's unexpected and changes your life. So, like an anagram, we rearrange the message to the one with the new higher meaning that is probably opposite of what we thought it was.

Right now, many of us are waiting for a plan, this is a blatant sign that says we have to *move,* which means we have to be thumbed out on our own highway waiting for a dream to come by and get us. Dreams have plans of their own that demand flexibility. Sometimes it's not my plan that comes to be but some crazy idea that has not even come to fruition and says: *We're now going to be traveling and we will figure it out as we go.* One moment I'm working my ass off selling real estate and then in the midst of a pandemic escape from the city real estate boom, my entire business comes to a stop. Things slide into contract and I'm done for the moment. It becomes clear, it's time to publish this book. I have no idea where it's going, I just know I'm going with it.

In a manifestation mode, we must decide what the priority is. A younger me once read that to be rich, act rich. I decided back then to try on this motif, so I hung out at the most expensive places like I belonged there. I tried on designer outfits in department stores, I dined at the most expensive restaurants and ordered appetizers. I test-drove

luxury cars, planned extravagant vacations and felt what it was like to be rich. I even taped a cut-out of a Range Rover to my fridge. After doing a huge business deal, my brother visited us on a holiday, saw the photo, and weeks later mailed me a Range Rover brochure. I laughed, thinking he was playing with me for my paste-up, then opened the brochure to find a check for a new Range Rover. As children we always shared, when I got some, he got some, it never changed. Manifestations do work in weird ways.

After understanding the laws of manifestation being about what we focus on, I then realized that money is not the means to my happiness—being free to do what I love is. So, I decided to try that motif on and incorporate what I loved into my everyday life. I dreamt that I was free to do what I cherished and felt what it was like to own this pleasure. My excitement from imagining being in this state then overruled my reactions around the mundane things I wished I didn't have to do. Since I now had an appreciation for what was good in the pile of crap, the good feelings grew. I felt rich in ways that were important to me; like my ability to see beauty in nothing special because my dreams were showing it to me. Mind you, I still love to manifest abundant things and they arrive alongside my dreaming of a magical reality.

Our daydreams and night dreams come from the same place; they are spirit talking to us in the midst of our minds working out mental gibberish. One night I dreamt a gorilla was standing next to my husband, measuring that he was

taller. I dreamed I opened a store called The Infinity Shop, and I kept hearing: *"Remember this!"* We wake up and forget, so keep a pen and notebook by the bed to write down all the abstract pieces you remember. They might not make sense today because they're jigsaw fragments coming together that are huge messages with directives–just make a point to remember. Though if you don't, don't worry, they will keep coming around in different forms until you do. Take it seriously, own the fact that besides being human you're a dreamer and honor your dreams.

Funny, but sometimes my husband needs to pound his chest like a gorilla to be heard around me. I need to be aware that his gorilla is in the house and let him be, so he can shift into not having to pound his chest. The message is for me not to be overbearing. The Infinity Shop dream was telling me that my new business would have no barriers. Our conversations with the Universe offer us an opportunity to break an old spell and step into our wizardry to bring our dreams into existence. We must tap into a magical grid that's a mental wonderland where we go to plug in to possibilities. It's like going to an amusement park where we lose ourselves in moments of glee; this is a cerebral zone where what's rational doesn't matter. What matters is the gusto we get from our bliss, as a spark of excitement has legs. Consider this good feeling as a limb in communion with our heart and soul that's synapsing on a spiritual plane and geared to go off and running.

Our initial dream is a destiny with a legacy, while the

feeling that accompanies it builds the energy of creation around it that enchants it into being. All we have to do is allow the dream to evolve and chase where it's going like Alice running after the hare trying to capture the wonder of it. And when things get tight and scary, we dream our way out of it, or we do dream battle where we become the heroes of our dreams, and so what if we're playing with inspiration. Inspiration is a gift that pulls unfolding ideas out of our hat. Concepts born from our reveries expand when words partial to impossible don't matter.

I had a feeling something new was coming to be in my life, and I had no idea what or how it would unfold, just that it arrived and was unpacking its bags. Impressions that make zero sense are finding their way just like us. As the dreamers of this world, we must dream of the bigger picture. We must dream our way through turmoil, instill higher meaning into this evolution, and show up for what calls us. Thus, our imaginary speculations will hold us when we're lost; they will find us when we're between professions and change our directions when we're going the wrong way.

After all, we are additionally selfless dreamers where we dream for the world in service to humanity. Our planetary dreams balance the status quo of bad energy running the global body. To dream of peace and massive healings is assistance dreaming for the goodness of mankind. To wish well or vision well for someone we don't even know is an offering. To wish well even for someone who has it in for us, when they're stuck in their own darkness and need help is

charity. We must give something back to this gracious planet that is caring for us, as our appeal makes our hearts fit for use. All our struggles show us there is no us-and-them, we're all in the same boat. So, when one end of the boat gets too heavy, those with the strength to hold it up with higher wisdom will have to do so.

Reality is constantly turning life as we know it, to the unbelievable channel. Nobody knows what's real or false anymore, as security and certainty took a leave of absence. I consider not feeling safe a wake-up call that pushes us to come into our real power because we have to do something about it. This is a time to pull in the courage to stand with ourselves, move energy, and define what we will hold onto over any predicted future. It's about becoming an adversary with possibility over chance and having the mindset to become heedful to what's needed in the unfamiliar. People talk about the new normal, that's a lie, there is no normal we can bank on. The truth is we're being called to address what matters most, as crisis has a way of bringing us together with the new dream it needs—the one we can bank on.

The Good Witch is a dreamer; she finds her remedies in her dreams and visions and tracks her dreams for directions when life goes haywire. Bad Bitch is also a dreamer, but she's into dreamonizing. She tends to focus on the demons lurking in her dreams, the ones that are always trying to take her down. Are they real? They are when she feeds them. Her demons are the aspects of herself that get freaked out when they don't know what's going on and so she's in constant

battle with them. Good Witch yanks Bad Bitch out of her head to show her interesting things to distract her. The gifted visions wake her up, shake her off, and bring her back to dreaming her way around. The Good Witch is actually part of Bad Bitch's dream; she's empowering Bad Bitch to be a healer, a mystic, an Abracadabra Shaman who plays with loving realities in the midst of the harshness running on the polluted channels.

While dreaming, we might think we're dreaming of one thing, though our dreams are doing what's needed for us in our bigger life story. Our life stories are like tapestries that we're constantly weaving and sometimes we have to drop a stitch to get odd pieces to connect, or we have to undo sections of what we've done prior. We might think there's a process—there is none. Dream movement is accelerated by heartfelt stirrings, while our life stories are one big dream intertwining together with consciousness that's connected to who we are in spirit. The only time we're really lost is when we lose our spirit connection and then the dream becomes about getting it back. If we're lacking love, we must entwine it into the pattern, so piece by piece we add the ingredients to weave our dream along. The dream becomes the guide that pulls everything together and all we have to do is keep dreaming.

Dream Weaving:

- Our dreams run across live-wire gridlines that attract self-activating dynamics, pulling what's needed into their paradigm to manifest.
- Once all the dream ingredients are collected, our willingness to believe in these dreams is our passport to start moving with them.
- Be open to traveling with a dream while it collects itself.
- As on The Yellow Brick Road, when we cross paths with a dark energy that wants to kill our dream, know that dreams geared toward higher intentions and service are protected.
- A good dream will not die but will keep coming around to manifest.
- We must honor our dreams as sacred journeys.
- We don't have to know where we're going in a dream, for we're exploring consciousness.
- Our dreams demand the courage to make us strong enough to carry them.
- Always allow your dreams free rein; never confine them with reality. They require space and free will to build upon themselves in order to accumulate energy, which creates the magnetic field that attracts more energy.
- Once dreams are full of magnetism, they bleed into real life, and override what's no longer needed.

- Dreams push us to grow with them, always taking us to the next level.
- You can dream your way out of anything or into something, but you have to be available to go to the edge of everything.
- Our dreams will tell us what they want from us.
- A dream has its own agenda, which is how it becomes life changing.
- Dreams orchestrate a higher way of living, making us lighter as we lift off our heaviness.
- Dreams deliver gifts that are hidden in symbols to keep us on our toes.
- We might think we're being sidetracked, but it's the dream expanding our perceptions.
- Sometimes we feel depressed, but in truth we have not dreamed enough.
- Soul-searching in a dream elevates us beyond what's actually happening in reality.
- Never let reality get in the way of your dreaming, just honor it as past energy created.
- Dreams are miracles that go beyond the conditioning of what's possible.
- When a dream is going around the bend, it means a new reality is being created.
- Dreams incite us to be all that we've ever imagined. Spotlighting our potential, they crack an opening into it.

- The obstacles, hard work, and learning experiences around a dream are part of its magic, so not only is our dream coming to fruition—we're coming to fruition with it.
- A dream will push us out of where we were—and, like a birth, push us through darknesss into a new way.
- When fears arise in dream, it's a message that we're strong enough to conquer them.
- A dream brings us into the unknown and demands that we delve into the mystery of life.
- A good dream will ask us to decide whether we can live life without our dream.
- When an important decision needs to be made, dream on it.
- Dreaming about sustenance amidst chaos brings beneficence.
- Think about who is dreaming the dream and know that it's the God essence of who we are that holds our creativity and is just passing it over to us.
- As a dream is manifesting, miracles happen, and this is how we know it's manifesting.
- On an adventurous dream, remember we're holding hands with our spirit.
- As we dream, there's no such thing as failure—it's just some obstacles that are a twist on our way to success.
- Everything we dream of is an ingredient that wants to be part of what we're weaving, or it wants to be

untangled if it's all knotted up, or even removed if it's no good anymore.

- Our imagination directs us beyond belief to new beliefs.
- Dreams are a turning point.
- We create our dreams and then they recreate us.
- To live our dream: the first step is to walk with faith, the second step is to acknowledge we are carrying a gift, and the third step is offering it to the world.

Love Life

Welcome to love's lessons; this is a lifelong course where signing in is unnecessary since we're all here on celestial scholarships. There are no fees or velvet ropes, so take off your shoes and put down your bags—you don't need them in this reality. Intimacy doesn't care if you close your eyes or keep them open, just don't run away when love pierces your heart. Many have spent a lifetime looking for love, as love can be elusive for those looking for it. Enticed by our readiness, seduced by aspirations, it will break down doors to get to us and may suddenly come up behind us and pull so hard on our coattails that we fall to the ground. Love runs its own show and calls the tunes. There are no rules or boundaries with love, you can't make it happen or tell it to leave, it follows the scent of our heart's yearning. So, adorn yourself as the seducer or seductress of enchantments—we were made for this apprenticeship.

Our lessons of love open all locked doors, smashing barriers and breaking open concepts. When I was in my late teens, my first true love unexpectedly passed away and I thought I would die of heartbreak, as all I wanted was to follow this great love to heaven. As time passed, I lived with

severe grief in a loveless state like a zombie. One day I began to get dressed again and stepped back into myself even though I was broken-hearted and limping along in constant tears. I had stopped hiding my true self and the light of this action attracted an angel of a being who arrived to show me that love lives on and comes in many forms.

This new love also knew of my first love; it was obvious they were of the same vibration and it felt as if my new love was sent to me by my lost love. We had a son who one day demanded to play the drums; my first love was a drummer and I wondered if he had come back to me as my child. When I was pregnant, a psychic said, “You will have a boy who knows love and will play the drums, he will change the world.” He did, he changed my world in ways that banged truths back into my being.

Some people are not easy. I am one of the not-easy ones who will not stand in a loveless state. I demand love and once love arrives, it’s in charge. Love is not delicate and will shake us to the bones as once instilled inside us it rips away everything that’s not love. When you think it’s gone, suddenly it comes back around in disguise, because it’s always the same original love that we had the moment we took our first breath. It doesn’t replace itself; it just manifests in different forms to pound the doors of our hearts back open. Love will smash our ego to smithereens, reflecting on all discrepancies that hold it away. It demands that we feel all the parameters of pain in order to transcend beyond what’s not love. In the end, we’ll see our suffering as part of our

coming home to love, so every failure, all the heartbreak and all the pain, is about a return to love.

The ceremony is to love love—and the ritual around this is in the knowing that love exists somewhere in everything. That's a hard concept, to get that there is love in hellish experiences, though when we question where, we mostly find it hiding in our broken heart. On that day after a huge brawl at my first real estate company, I questioned my friend who instigated an explosive episode by complaining to my manager when I told him the truth about his house, that it wasn't worth what he wanted. When I asked him why he caused such trouble, he said he did me a big favor and I was lucky to be out of there. It took a few months to realize he actually did do me that favor, as I needed a change. I also needed to no longer have friends like him. I didn't plunge from that experience but survived. I even felt a distant love for my ex-friend who caused it and thanked him in spirit.

The reason a closed heart hurts so much is because it has lost faith in love. Every time we go to the Hate Café, get revenge or play in the *I Have to Win* sandbox, we're closing the door on love. Maybe we've been spurned, though holding someone in contempt while looking down on their actions, we might see that they're reeling in severe grief, so untangling from our opinions takes time. We're burning love karma, the flame that removes all that blinds us from not seeing love. Our stepping away from these broken feelings takes great strength, especially in a culture that propagates hatred, being right, and getting even. Every step

away from our place of darkness is the beginning of our walk back to love. This journey might take us through the mud where we totally lose ourselves; once we understand that our pain is part of our healing, we stop beating ourselves up and begin to heal.

Love karma must be worked out with the people we love that drive us crazy, as the difficult ones are the exact relationships we burn up karma with. Once the karma is burned up, all that's left is love. My mother and son are the ones I've burned love karma with. It's hard, it sucks, and it's a total gift. If we have to do this breakdown of ego with someone, it might as well be with someone we love. My mother tortured me for years, causing trauma and guilt. In the end, her actions pushed me through everything that held me back from being my own She-ro. It happened that way because I used her as my catalyst for growth, as after being a wounded victim, I never got lost in that story. Instead, I blew myself into a new story as her dark side turned on my light side because I bid it to do so. She taught me to be the opposite of her, while taking on her assets. I always imagine meeting her in the afterlife, as we slap each other five on a job well done.

As far as my son goes, our relationship is strong and comes from way back, probably from lifetimes ago where we've worked things out together. He's a teacher who challenges my every action and way of thinking that goes off course. The lessons are sometimes harsh and painful, as he never holds back. He's also a truth slayer so everything that is

not of the highest accord with him is smacked down. My ego has bowed to his wisdom as he rightfully sees useless discrepancies and describes them. We battle when I'm in resistance, though we transcend our battles by never getting lost in any of it, other than the love and respect we have for each other. To see the stories we share as coming from love, the pain as breaking down what's not love, our growth as love in action, is to understand that barriers are lies we believe in must be obliterated. It's rare to find someone who will do this with you, who will stand with you and demand that you don't fall into the cracks of your own bullshit. That's love!

I decided that I'm here to use everything happening as grist for my mill, as not to would leave me lost in stories I don't want to be stuck in. Since I didn't design this plan, I concede that on some level I agreed to be part of it seeing that I'm here. During the times I feel like I'm in a bad movie and the darkness is out to get me, it's from there that my faith runs out and my new directive is about getting it back. These are the exact occasions that hold openings for enlightening breakthroughs. Yes, I agree, it sucks that we have to go through this torture to be free, but the choice is to either go across with what's happening or go down with it.

A woman who lost her twenty-three-year-old daughter to an overdose said that if she met God, she would kill him. This dear woman is my relative and her daughter is my niece. I understand her anger and pain and still grapple with this great loss that has shredded our family. Though I don't want

to kill God, at times I have forsaken even the concept of any God whatsoever and have screamed to the ethers, "How could you let this happen?" After the anger subsides into pain, I just want to understand. This desire to make sense out of what seems so senseless might be a waste of time, though it brings me to a place of love for my niece where I will still fight for her.

In the beginning of grieving her loss, I felt her essence talking to me through this experience of Hell, reminding me of past joys and all the happiness she brought forth. My higher self feels that if I can come to a place of peace around this loss, I am offering it back to her. It's hard as the lessons mainly about forgiveness arrive. These lessons feel like a hammer striking my inability to tolerate all the wrongs, even in myself, and they strike until I shatter. The healing and coming back to love is a process, where one day I find I'm so changed that I have no idea who I am and I don't care.

I have said hello to darkness and offered it love. This darkness soon after stopped grabbing me and honored my dedication to holding love as I passed. We get knocked down and it's love on some level that gets us up again to teach us how to walk in new ways. So, stand in love, take baby steps back to love, believe in love, be loving even when you want to scream. We do this as a practice that spits in the face of hatred, of disappointment, of hopelessness. We can love from across the street, from beyond this reality into the heavens, and through time into past lifetimes. A love dynamic pulls us away from hatred and disappointments,

right back to love. It's the prodding action to *Click Your Ruby Slippers* into love that ignites the love that we've had all along. This love is telling us to stop wandering around looking for it—it's telling us to stand still and call it home.

I do love the force of God, not the man in the robe, but the feeling that there is something bigger than me out there that has got me covered. A knowing that in prayer there is a listening and a fulfillment. Where exactly it comes from, I don't know. I just know. In ceremony I honor this God force and value it and even when I get angry at it I feel there is still always a deep love there for me if I want it. I want it. That's why there is a connection, because I reach for love into the beyond and it delivers. It's a decision I made way back, that since I am here, *I will stay in love.*

In ceremony we decide if we're moving in love or fear, in love or anger, in love or depression. In ceremony, we commit to what love is about over all else and the moment we reach for it, we're embraced. Bad Bitch has been captured by love and instead of it making her all airy-fairy, it's made her more discerning. She's got no time to dally in places beneath her summit and has dumped all her emotional baggage to get there. Good Witch bypasses bullshit and goes right to where applause exists, as she's sparking the magic of complimenting what she finds tasteful. It's a ritual of homage to what's enchanting and as we swat away all that's not captivating, we move from our old-minded rigmarole into what's naturally bewitching.

The three stepping stones to love are . . .

1. Don't align anywhere where love is not.
2. Peruse all the aspects of where love is.
3. Question it.

Akin to the question: *Does This Bring Me Joy?* Instead we ask ourselves: *Can this lead to love?* The answer to this question appears in neon as it guides us to find love in all the aspects we have overlooked. Is there love in a friend's struggles even when they're being difficult? Is there love in the feeling of I don't belong here? Is there love in heartbreak, in shame, in rejection? Is there love when we're done agreeing with what's wrong? It depends on where these things push us to go, for when we show up for ourselves no matter what—it's love. Showing up for love is doing serious soul-searching to realize that love is missing, and we can't live without it. It's when we admit we don't have it, when we give up on seeking it, and turn toward our hearts to revive it that we find it!

An old friend I worked for who said he loved me, dropped the love the moment I requested to be paid accordingly. Love is not confined to sweet *la-di-da* times; it's more alive than ever in hard times saying: *I'm here, use me!* We have to show up for what's harsh, to speak out, to take a stand, and to do damage control. Doing what it takes, we might lose false-love, self-centered friends, business that doesn't pay, and the parts of us that have no confidence. Allowing this loss as a way of honoring self-love, completes us.

Self-love is the voice that will not shut up. It's our inner strength that's gathering our forces after we've been slammed and the push to keep going. Self-love is a gracious kind of love that our divine spirit holds for us when we've dropped love off at the curb as we enter the bar to drown our sorrow. Self-love is the understudy that steps in when we've forgotten our lines, when we've lost hope, when our mojo has run off and we indulge in self-pity. Self-love will grab us back into love's arms the moment we accept ourselves—the moment we bless where we are—and when we acquiesce to enmesh with the essential part of our self that knows Love Rules!

Love rules:

- Loving ourselves attracts love, as love is attractive.
- If you're not feeling the love, connect with your divine spirit and request a love map.
- To love an illness, an enemy, a painful experience, forces all things to give us their gifts.
- Loving what's hard is not easy—but neither is breaking open a rock to find a diamond.
- While others throw hate bombs, we throw back love bombs.
- Recognize the loving place that exists, for seeing the love enhances it.
- Even only if love is mostly being enhanced in just us, once we are full, it bleeds over.

- Fighting for love is a waste of time–fighting for the ability to love is valuable.
- Sometimes we're supreme assholes, but love does not judge, it waits for understanding.
- A piercing moment will come when we remove the splinter and no longer walk in pain.
- Be yourself, even if you're selfish and at your worst, as we need to own all aspects of ourselves in order to surrender them and love ourselves through it.
- When we love ourselves as we are, we soften. A door opens and maybe a bunch of little monsters run out, but there we are, a beautiful soul awakening from a bad dream.
- The more we wake up to embrace love, the more love abounds.
- We swim in the love we own.
- We receive what we believe we deserve.
- If we don't believe we deserve love, but keep giving it anyway, the belief in lack can no longer hold up.
- We might be weird and not fit the format, but this is also sublimely attractive to others who are the same way, as love is the enchantment of like kind energy.
- It takes courage to love in the midst of animosity; it's the gift of loving that matters.
- Love is never an accident; even when it fails, it's always a lesson.

- Love is holding someone's happiness when they can't do it for themselves. She or he will know where to come for it when they're ready.
- Love that's betrayed will die a hideous death, but our spirits remain intact, and when we honor our spirit, it will heal our broken hearts and bring us back to love.
- Love transforms everything and has no boundaries, though this doesn't mean we must sit in the mud with what's unloving—unless we're growing our own lotus through it.
- When unloving voices come online to warn us about all the illusions that want to drag us down, tell these voices you love them, as this freaks them out, so they shut up.
- Not loving is a burden to be dropped, so drop it in order to live in a love zone.
- The choice between love and hate determines whether we grow or wither.
- Play with being loving no matter what and see how the energy shifts around you.
- Love will hold us when we've disappeared.
- Love is all that ever matters.
- Love is all we have to offer.
- Being endless and eternal, love is the gift we leave behind.
- Love leaves a trail that leads everywhere.

- Even when you have to pretend to love, you are still sparking love.
- Even when love doesn't work, love anyway.
- Love is who you are in retaliation to it all.
- Follow love's rules, because they will take you where love matters most—they will pick you up and put you back where you belong.
- In the name of love, everything rises when we rise.

Healing . . .

My heart was making demands, yelling: "*Stop trying to shield me, I need to break open, and if this causes you pain, you must bear it.*" At the time, I was wrestling the tipping point and was losing as intense experiences kept coming until all my cover-ups no longer worked. Forced to surrender into the depths of my pain, I stopped fighting. When this happened, Bad Bitch catapaulted into a healing of herself that went beyond many lifetimes. There was an angel with me, for when my grief became too much, I had tried to leave this world and this cosmic angel took my hand and pulled me through. I had gone to the other side and come back, when at sixteen years old I danced on the edge like The Fool in the Tarot deck, he was lost in a reverie, while I fell off in a crash and came back as an empowered bitch. No wonder I had no censor, God doesn't either.

The Good Witch knows you cannot throw a spell on a climactic sequence of events. You can't protect yourself, nor can you live too carefully because traumas are not in our control. All we can do when a crisis hits is to go into survival mode. Distress is the teacher I abhor, the one that hits you with a ruler, fails you, and ruins your life, until you realize

you're better than it. We're only better when we decide to survive and heal. It's normal to hate our teachers, to argue it out while we're in the process of breaking down our ego to get to radical acceptance. The surrender is the turnaround, which is not to say we should ever give up. No, never give up! Still, we accept that we can't move further until we get our consciousness upped to the next higher ante, because transformation has its own rules that hold miracles.

It's obvious this lifetime is not for the faint of heart: it's a battlefield, a jungle where we're rolling along fine, then suddenly we're slammed. We're not lambs going to slaughter, we have useful tools and weapons that not many are aware of. Think about the cosmic energy field, I did during the viral epidemic that swept our planet. I went into meditation and called the virus forth to have a conversation. I asked it what it ultimately wanted, and it said it didn't want to be here as much as humanity didn't want it here. It was then that I realized it was not the enemy, per se, but a lost aspect of dark energy that got stuck here and needed help to move out.

In meditation, I went higher up to the heavens and called forth the medicine spirits; I saw them sitting in a circle and joined them. They were sitting around an opening in the cosmos and sending huge light down to our planet and then pulling it back up. I looked into the opening to see our beautiful Earth surrounded in light, being washed by this descending and uplifting energetic motion. This went on a while, until the medicine spirits then sent down healing

vibrations. I knew this healing had a life of its own and would bring some of humanity home to heaven, as it was their time once again to know heaven where eventually they would be invited to join the healers. I saw this scenario as clearly as day and knew I was encouraged to help by sitting in this healing circle as often as I would remember to.

As far as remembering goes, recognize that you agreed to this specific undertaking, agreed to this wild ride, agreed to being on a spiritual quest while in human form, and agreed to constantly being shattered while being part of an immense healing shift through all of it. So, when shit storms are knocking us over, it means we were ready to process out our own equivalent darkness, to move it out, and become lighter. Sometimes it's not even our own crap, we were just going along and passed through a dark zone and got covered in it. There are no mistakes around here, as our job is to clean up the darkness flying around as a service to humanity.

This is a wake-up time, a time to look at the bigger picture, a time to pay attention and to decide what we believe in. More importantly, it's a time to define how we will stand with ourselves. Standing for healing, against violence, with hope for a promising future is a powerful stance. We must live the message we want to share. In the beginning, things may get worse when healing. All the symptoms flare to be addressed, as this is a healing crisis. This is not a passive time, and even if the crisis is not happening directly to us, it has everything to do with us. Right now, we are either healing ourselves, assisting in

healing others, or here to heal this planet. If you think you're not part of it, you will soon realize you are, and the sooner you do, the better you will be.

I wonder, when I'm selling houses and suddenly the negotiations turn to ego and greed, what do I have to do with it? I'm smack in the middle, usually getting slimed by both parties, while Bad Bitch screams that she's done dealing with these low-level experiences. Meanwhile, Good Witch moves untainted through these storms by transforming herself through them, so she leaves a healing trail. The evolved mannerism is: *Go to your Holy land and quickly process the dreck out. Hold thumbs out and up for our boons to roll in from the mystery zone, and never get lost in the mire for more than a few minutes.*

It often feels like we're not in charge, though we always have a say. How many times have we sidestepped grander knowledge, thinking we knew better, only to find out there's no escape exit and the only way out is through? Our scars are bookmarks noting that the sacred stories we've owned are all worthy tales that hold space for the light to enter. Never erase these stories and use your say-so to keep adding your dreams to them. We're always in the process of opening ourselves to the grace that's around the next corner—just get to the corner, even if you have to crawl there.

I once saved a feral kitten's life and named her Angel. She acts like she's in the jungle and in constant danger in my living room. Sometimes, when I am petting her, she can't take it and nips at my hand to stop. She remembers that

someone once put her in a plastic bag and took her to a kill shelter, so the sound of a crinkling plastic bag terrifies her. I have a nice collection of cloth bags now and am gentler than I have ever been. These furry friends are teachers on healing trauma. I love her and slowly she is surrendering to love and lying next to me, purring and giving me her belly to rub as I write. I called her Angel to remind myself that being involved in the things that are not easy is where so many gifts are hidden. I was once the feral bitch who, in naming myself Good Witch, could heal. We attract what we are!

It's no longer a secret that we have the power to heal ourselves on every level, though we are doing this in tandem with our divine spirit and often we are not doing it in this dimension. It's a matter of focus, dedication, and faith in the idea that we'll come back to wellness no matter what. Again, it might not be in this dimension. We have to stop backing away from our healings and agree that we're not at the beck and call of mortals. First, we have to take our remedial cure on the higher plane.

My best results have come out of synchronicities that are direct missives from conversations with my inner witch doctor. I have named her Shouting Mountain, since many times she yells remedies into my mind at unexpected moments, like the time she screamed "CHAGA!" into my ear during a yoga class. I had no idea what Chaga was. It turned out to be a mushroom with the perfect antidotes for an affliction I was dealing with. Books have fallen off shelves and tinctures have called out to me. People I've crossed paths

with have led me to the perfect healers who practice radical energy medicine and create miracles. Strangers have said mind-shifting things in odd places. One piece of the puzzle leads to another as faith in healing is my objective. While I converse with the otherworld, with my ancestors and divine spirit, there's nothing that can block a healing, once requested. The key is: We must desire, ask, invite, hunt for, and command our healings.

On the days when I can bless the difficulties as part of the healing needed, I give in to the limitations, understanding that there are none and that I have just been directed to try another way. How many times did Alice have to grow bigger or smaller to fit through a keyhole, to get to the next place? Like Alice, we've all fallen down a rabbit hole. We can have conversations with a deck of cards, ask directions from a caterpillar smoking a pipe, or just go chasing after Tweedle Dee. Once we get it that we're in a magical realm, we can laugh at the Queen who's shouting, "Off with their heads!" We can communicate with animals, plants, spirits, and all the magic that exists. We can kiss and make up without even speaking. We can heal, release, and overcome without moving our bodies. We can play with energy and chains of thought, which is much more fun than dealing with what we think we know.

Since we're in times of great change, trying to hold on to things is not an option. The vibration of radical change is happening to move us off our toadstools, and if we're in communion with a higher source we will receive signs. I hear

confirmations that these shifts that feel like turmoil lead to a bold newness that's coming to be. I've received directions of what to do and even in the darkest moments, I've heard the message: *The darkness is not endless, but a path back to the light.* Radical change demands intrinsic trust, especially when time warps, and nothing makes sense. How crazy that we have to trust the signs while living in a reality that looks like a world gone mad? The signs and messages are a lifeline that come in dreams, in circumstances, and in our awake perceptions.

During a recent time, when I had changed lanes and everything that was working prior had stalled, I was not sure how I would manifest my sustenance. One night, I dreamt that I was about to give birth; the doctor in the dream was telling me to push and I forcefully said, "No, I'm not ready." This actually happened to me back when I actually did give birth. I wasn't ready and stupidly listened to a doctor who was in a hurry to get to the golf course. I pushed to exhaustion and in the end my baby was pulled out with forceps. Luckily he was fine but I was not and had to heal.

In the dream, I was in control and said: *No, I'm not pushing until I'm ready.* I woke up and realized I was giving birth to this book and coming close to the end of being done. The message was: *Don't Push.* I then pulled a Tarot card, the Queen of Pentacles, which declared that I have what it takes to create prosperity in all its forms: beauty, wealth, love, and a happy home. This card symbolizes fertility. I innately knew that all would be well, so no need to push, as not pushing but allowing is a new way of being for

me.

During a time when I was sinking into despair, I was instructed to do a three-day reset, the reason being that the more magic we are part of, the more magic is part of us. I was directed to drink a lot of water and eat lightly; no alcohol, no questioning myself, no negative thoughts, no fear, no hooking into darkness, just three days of flowing with magic only. It worked, and in three days, even though nothing in the exterior world had changed, my essence and vitality came back online and once again I was back in my groove.

Our groove is the circuit that is paving our way so on the days we're not in it, we must sidestep our way back to it. Music always helps me; I sing at the top of my lungs in the car, in the shower, in the living room, as I'm doing whatever it takes to get back to my mental garden. It might take a day of reading books; a day hanging out on a beach, maybe I stay in bed till dinner, have a heart-to-heart conversation, or a good cry. I find sitting in meditation when we are gyrating, or writing out dreams and asking for what we want, helps.

As far as Bad Bitch is now going, I have deemed that she is no longer one who is not good in any manner or degree. She's not morally reprehensible, nor does she have one inch of an evil or wicked character. Like many women in the hip-hop community who call themselves bad bitches, she's an empowering force who knows what she wants and has gone from the aspect of being really bad to being quite good. Accordingly, she's now bad in the sense of being great, because

she's healed herself of connotations and even when she slips, she's still good a.k.a bad, as owing to her badass self, she cleans up her shit. Hence, I follow her into the living room as she turns up Michael Jackson on the stereo while singing, "*Because I'm bad, I'm bad, come on, you know I'm bad.*" I often think of my mother saying, "You're only good when you're sleeping" and I know there's nothing left to heal on that statement–it's done!

And last, even when reality is painful, we must stay in our hearts to get through it. Our heartland is an integral niche that defines our principles and the place where we are truly fearless and strong. It's the place we come home to, the zone where we're not wimps but matriarchs who know right from wrong, and all we have to do is be good to ourselves. Herein we embrace all of ourselves and offer gratitude for our restoration even before it arrives.

In the moments when I feel off, I hug myself and say, "*You are doing great!*" Because even when I feel weird and the world is on a crazy roll, I'm here doing my best and that is great. Our heartland grabs us to pull us into sacred ceremony where we bow to our healing, our love, our dreams, our kindred ties, our business, and our residence here. Our rituals of gratitude around these gifts instill grace, so the blessings come. We define the moment when we decide that we're not being slayed but are healing what slays us. We decide to live in our power–and this is our offering.

Healing Notions:

- Close your eyes, travel the cosmos, and ask for a healing. Ask for directions and antidotes, and pay attention to what comes, and any random things you hear and find—there's no request that ever goes unanswered.
- In the moments before the answers come, move into your power place, your heartland. It's from here that you can translate what you see into higher knowing.
- Stepping into a sacred zone is like flipping a switch—a realization is all it takes and we're in. Here our thoughts matter most, so if you can't direct them, turn them off and wait.
- Notice what doesn't fit into your highest aspects when you're where you don't belong.
- Our intuitive way knows that uncertainty is an adventure.
- Healing is personal, as it goes layers deep to unearth old assumptions and drag them up for transformation.
- In a healing mode, we drop connotations on bad aspects—using old ways to grow out of.
- We must figure out how to unravel our emotional wounds or decide if we need to let them just pass. Sit with the issue until you get a true feeling. Wait for it, you'll know, then follow your feeling.

- We must clear away all that's been imposed upon us to reveal our own beliefs and then decide which conclusions have enough levitation to elevate us.
- We're never alone on a healing journey and closer to spirit than ever. Remember your spirit partnership and take the invisible hand that's reaching out to guide you.
- During times we're surrounded by darkness we're being called to shine our light where we are, as the panacea we offer illuminates the power of healing returning to us.
- Whenever I've struggled with wellness, miracles happened each time I dedicated my healing cause to an outcome that included my service to humanity.
- Being in service to a greater cause calls all healing forces to action.
- Even when we consider that there's a greater cause that we don't yet know, just thinking about it enamors it to define itself.
- As we fill our minds with healing thoughts, we attract them.
- Focus on the reasoning for why we want to be well and what we'll do once we are.
- Delve into the expressions we use for the characteristics of symptoms, like: *This situation is killing me, it's a pain in the ass, it's backbreaking, I can't take it*—and then work on mentally changing the offset around these feelings.

- We're being called to become heroes who survive the most searing stories because heroes are role models who carry other wounded beings across.
- "I survived!" or "I'm surviving!" are huge power statements.
- Even to survive a good death is valid, as a good death is a gift that we agree to have when the time comes. Imagine going out with a smile on your face, it's possible if we have lived with that smile inside.
- Tap into the way that shows you the way.
- Have the courage to surrender when you can't control the wheel, because we know we're in the hands of a greater force that's driving.
- Once we come to peace around what is, the narration shifts, and the real healing begins.
- Yes, it's difficult coming to peace around painful experiences, but we need to go deep into what the pain is saying in order to understand what to do about it.
- We must let the disturbance be acknowledged in order to heal it.
- See afflictions as turning points, telling us that something's out of balance.
- Maintain your highest disposition when doing healing work.
- Bad Bitch, when losing her standing, never fell into a victim mode, instead she excavated a new standing as Good Witch.

- Always dream your way out when you're locked in.
- The Universe has its stories that we revolve in, but it's up to us what we do inside these narratives. Once we get that we're invited to create inside the Universe's creation, we're in union with our magic no matter where the story goes.
- It's always about the bigger picture, which hides among the details being portrayed.
- Approach impressions with the intent to see beyond all that appears to be. Once we've touched upon this concept, we're pulled into a wisdom zone.
- Always clear communication lines of static and pay serious attention to directions.
- Often our healing happens in night dreams, also known as night school. We wake up knowing a shift has happened. After one of these experiences, move slowly to incorporate the new frequencies. These astral trips might leave you feeling disoriented because you've been rearranged, so don't try to be who you were—just let it be so you can see who you are now.
- We've all arrived with the antidotes—and all the solutions we need are in our medicine bags—they're imaginary.

PART THREE

LIVING OUR BAD BITCH–GOOD WITCH MAGIC

"Synchronicity is a confirmation that we are smack in our magic."

During a period of transition, I was reminded that my Earth birth was a passage from a heavenly dimension to this denser reality. Sometimes we're between the here and there and we feel lost. I did. In this particular shift, it was as though I was running between bases as fast as I could to get to the next base but wasn't going anywhere. One morning during this time, while I was writing my three Artist's Way pages (a creative writing program designed by Julia Cameron) I asked the Universe for a miracle. I was writing about what was going on, when I took a break to open my Facebook page, and the first post I read said: *In the process of losing and finding ourselves, over and over, we discover our magic.* This resonated as deep truth and I wondered who wrote it. I put on my glasses and saw that I wrote this quote in my last *Abracadabra* book and a friend who was leading a yoga retreat in Tulum had posted it.

Synchronicity, is it a coincidence or a direct message with magical interludes from the Universe? Amazing how when

we feel lost, we lose touch with who we are and by asking for a miracle, one arrives and brings us right back to the fact that we're not lost. I realized I was smack in the space where I'm once again discovering new alchemy. I then knew I had to stop running, seeking, trying, and just be in the moment. Quickly, a new message came in that said: *The Universe has your back–align with it!* I immediately fell into a heavenly state to realize we create our own denser realities with fear-based emotions.

Inevitably, during the times when we don't know what's going on or when we're in a discomfort zone, it's important to know that we're closer to and more in our star endowment than ever. I call this a period of harsh magic, where we're not comfortable as things shift, while our new magic is being downloaded. It's the pause where we must stop the doing and tap into our innovative trust fund, being our natural bounty. To access its zone we must relax, ease back, and trust what's enticing in this birth canal. If we struggle we get stuck, and when we relax we slide right through.

Relaxing in turmoil is a great practice. It doesn't mess with the turmoil but says: *I'm just going to chill while you do what's necessary for our greater good.* Mind you, Bad Bitch decided to do this in retaliation to being slayed after every maneuver she tried, failed. Instead she went into humble mode and waited. Shortly thereafter, her Good Witch aspect stepped in, slapped her on a broom, and off she went to rise above it all.

In this particular transition, I was being challenged to own my creative potential along with integrity as a boundary. I was involved in a business deal with some really shady characters whom I had decided to step away from. Mind you, in twenty years I had never not finished closing a deal. This was a first, as my peace of mind became more important to me than the deal. I could have used the money, but everything felt wrong and not magical. Then again, shut-downs, turnarounds, and brush-offs are secretly way magical, as they're realigning us with a new vibration.

At this time, it was difficult to imagine my future the same way I'd always done. It came to me that the reason was that I could no longer do things in the same ways, expecting different results (the definition of insanity). It also came to me that by doing different things, I would still get the magical results I always have. I just didn't happen to know what those different things were yet, when I heard: *Go Right, Go Write!* The Universe definably has a sense of humor, because I have one. All that we are is what is a match for us, so when I ask for gifts, I get them, as I believe that I'm one of God's gifts.

I then knew my writing about the transition from Bad Bitch to Good Witch was now a priority, because I was channeling messages to myself from my highest self. These messages would be a guiding force to slide me though this changeover into where I would now live in full integrity. Full integrity does not judge but defines our way where nothing in the past matters, just being wholly in the now matters.

The first blink on our shift is a sense of relief. The second blink is a feeling of bliss. The third blink is that we take responsibility for our quality of life. Though, in reality, we might not actually be anywhere that denotes bliss, but bliss is an inside job. How crazy that we have to consider the chicken before the egg, our bliss before its existence? Taking responsibility for our liveliness is about our commitment to the new life design plan we create in tandem with the Universe.

Can we find bliss in dark times? We must! In-breath hope/out-breath fear, with dreams as our guide. As a child, books were how I escaped into other stories, I went to my room and left the world. After that I made up my own stories and could leave the world wherever I was. As we grow up, we get trapped in the rules and the schedules, I never did. The escape route is to delve into supreme moments of bliss wherever was can find it—and if it doesn't exist, we make it up. Suddenly we're jolted by a force of divine objective, a download trigger that moves us. We could be seasoning in our bed during a quarantine, chugging ice cream and watching Netflix, when suddenly we're up marching for our beliefs (even in spirit), because we have been called. It might look like we're doing some weird shit during a dark time, like looking for bliss while our city is being looted, but we're actually retrieving ourselves.

I stop to smell the roses, which saves me from escaping into denial, being unconscious, and not accepting actuality. Instead it's about appreciating a hit of pleasure because I

need one to keep going. Speaking of pleasure, someone from L.A. where marijuana is legal, sent me a marijuana vape pen called Bliss. I took one puff and fell into a free-fall of gloom. What the heck? I realized that manufactured bliss is bullshit, and we can't use it as an escape or to make what is crap better when it will always be crap, so I threw it in the garbage. Bliss has to be salvaged from a place where it really exists and has moxie–not in a vape pen.

I did hope for a puff of instant bliss but am glad that it didn't work because on the day I took the puff, I was feeling pretty delicate and it enhanced that feeling, leaving me to fend for myself, which I did. As I was spiraling, I had to grab myself into a bear hug and find something that had fortitude to hold onto, and this brought up the fact that I have valor. We all do! It's only a matter of whether we exercise it or not. I will fight for myself dauntlessly if I have to, even when I have to give up. For instance, if there's a message from the Universe saying: *Go chill out,* then I will chill with total audacity.

The Universe loves us as much as we love ourselves and treats us as well as we treat ourselves. Shifting means we must implement the concept of a higher progression over what's happening and step into it. It's shocking what we go through to finally get back to the hub of who we are. We have lost our minds, felt hopeless, followed the masses into a social media stupor, lain around in victim consciousness, railed against God, and succumbed to such shock over what is going on that we're hysterical or severely depressed. These dark places we find ourselves in are actually attracting huge

light, as a yin/yang duality is actually complementary in nature.

How it's complementary is that distribution seeks balance, so what appears to be disturbing is really duality coming back into its whole self. Therefore, being that nothing is ever completely one way, the word crisis (a word in the Chinese language that signifies danger and opportunity) is really about transformation. When we reject our crises, we stay stuck and no longer grow. By finding our power through the crisis, we find what's meaningful in it.

To acknowledge a yin/yang balance is to understand patterns like a Fibonacci sequence, where everything returns to its source. Since the nature of all things is to evolve, things will wobble when absorbing a shock and then process it out. What's happening now is that we've absorbed a shock and we're processing out all that no longer serves us in the highest way. We are wobbling, which doesn't mean we are falling–it means we are once again rising, maybe we're shaky, but getting ready to stand and walk in a new way. We're on the rebound, but when slammed to your knees, don't get lost on the way down, instead delve around for a holy perspective around faith and aspiration. Bad Bitch now knows better than to get lost in what's happening on the downside and to use it for all it's worth. Therefore, use the time, the pain, the grief, or whatever it is to cultivate a way to take the wisdom you need from this experience–and then figure out a way to come back stronger.

Toddlers wobble when they are learning to walk, they fall

down, laugh, cry, and get up again. Sometimes they crawl around on the floor for longer than expected and that's because they're fully in the experience of life on the floor and growing through it. Everything is always in the progression of coming back into balance, even when there's insanity and violence going on. It's especially during these times that we must create the space to pull in the opposite of violence, which is love, and we must sit with this love until we can get up again. In a world where there is so much pain and lack of consideration for the human race, we must do what we can to bring harmony back into symmetry.

A real estate client went on a tirade over a mistaken bedroom count on her listing. Meanwhile, there's serious suffering going on, the pandemic, an economic collapse, protests, and shootings. For a moment, I felt depressed that the balance was so off and then I grabbed myself back, because I am not feeding this wolf. The wolf story is attributed to a Cherokee Indian teaching his grandson about a fight that's going on between two wolves. One is evil and the other is good. The grandson asks, "Which wolf wins?" The grandfather replies, "The one you feed." The wolves, his grandfather tells him, are the different aspects of his mind.

In times of turmoil, everyone handles survival mode in their own way. Our values are flashing neon, our principles are checking themselves into rehab, our ego has been told to be quiet as we're gathering our wits about us, while figuring out where we are now—we're in uncharted territory. Since the unknown has arrived and the unexpected is the new

juncture, don't back away. Things are revealed when we stop calling the emergency hotline and get quiet enough to listen. Wait for some semblance of any significance, like a message saying: ***Honey, you are in life changing upheaval and your new job is to figure out a good next move.*** Once we get the message and stop gyrating around the changes being wrong, we can create an inner force to empower these changes. When I think about what the world now needs, I'm inspired to contribute.

Everything happening is either clearing something out or inviting something new in, so we need to make room for possibilities. Possibility will only prosper and grow in empty space. All else we have to do is have faith, which Don Miguel Ruiz, author of *The Four Agreements*, describes as believing 100%, without a doubt. My faith isn't in a fix-it program, it's in the knowing that I will do what's right for myself in any situation. If that means walk away, I'm gone. If it means there's something here, I roll up my sleeves, and when possibility is on the ticket, I'm invested. And sometimes I believe 100% without doubt in a force of invisible divinity that has my back and is guiding me. I hear things, that my son calls the voice.

We all have this ability to hear the voice, we've just haven't been trained that way. We get it mixed up with the hysterical mind that conveys anxiety statements, where the voice conveys power statements. The mind documents our state and once we begin to listen for it, the voice begins to speak. It may speak in feeling, in a push to go left, in a

desire, in a defining way that makes no sense now, but will later. We may not like the message, but the magic is in trusting it.

I was once stuck in a pattern where I was constantly doing business with either hysterical people losing their houses or greedy scavengers buying them. Suddenly, the dynamic during the pandemic flipped to greedy people selling or renting their houses at exorbitant prices to desperate people during desperate times. I did not want to be intervening within this story any longer, so I stopped. There I was, standing around with no work for a while. My husband, who has recorded hit rock-n-roll records since the eighties, told me that at the time when he decided to stop doing drugs, at first he had no work and then he began to work with the most amazing serious artists and his career went to the next level. We have to take a stand, draw a line as to where we can thrive, and believe that the Universe will meet us on the bridge to walk us across.

The Good Witch knows when it's time to exit and fly off on her broom, while fear and anxiety are screaming: *Get back here or we'll starve*! Since these emotions have shown up in protest, it's a message to starve fear and anxiety by not feeding them. It's time to decide if we're feeding our magic or the fear, the anger or the love, our depression or hope. We can't use our magic to make things safe or to protect the things that don't assist our highest good. Nor can we thrive by using our magic to manipulate things in our favor while forsaking others, as it will work against us. This way of being

will come back to bite our bitch ass and send us to the underworld, where we'll have to learn about integrity by beginning again.

Our plans have become all Looney Tunes, as suddenly we're in a reality we never surmised, but here we are. If you feel like you're in a Hell zone, it's time to cultivate some fascination out of the confusion. On the occasions we find ourselves slammed, it's because we get thrown to our knees for a reason. Finding ourselves on our knees is a very Holy posture where everything is now wavering in our favor for us to rise again in homage to what we worship. At first, we're in shock that things didn't work out, so we rant about it, then we keel over and cry. Next, we genuflect and then create our ensuing way. It happens this way because the Universe will always reflect what's needed for us to get going. Sometimes we're going away from our planned direction into a create-a-sphere—the space where we're suddenly inspired.

Nasty bitch weaved spells, took revenge, manipulated energy, and walked about with her ego out in front of her; she was flashing her wares and lost her mind. She was mostly mesmerizing until the day she became slayed by too much bravado. It happened because her kind of magic was defined by illusions and tricks and this is not the real magic I am speaking of. These days Bad Bitch still has opinions; she curses out car windows and wrestles with emotions, but finds herself stepping away from taking further action, as she's busy in conversation with her real magic. This magic is illuminatingly mystical and has spirit energy that wants to

bestow blessings. It will grab us to go in directions that make no sense but delivers so much wisdom that we can't be who we were any longer.

Once we tap into this magic, it takes on a life of its own, as it becomes active and starts working for us in the highest ways. So, when things don't make sense, we're in the mystical zone where there really is no right or wrong. It's more about just being in the experience and seeing what to take from it. Imagine that the opposite of what we think is happening is what's really happening–like we're not being screwed but instead unscrewing. How about we're not stuck, we're just unfastening from what no longer serves us. Every time I feel stuck, I realize I'm cemented in right-ology, as I think I know what's going on and that I know where I need to be going. I suddenly get it that my thoughts about the future are not always right, whereas being wrong is a directive that inexplicably means it's learning time, ego busting time, and turn-it-around holy time.

Souls always see the bigger picture; they are here with us in this crazy experience illuminating what's essential for us to spark on and leap off. Our souls are front and center when we've gone off the rails. They never give up on us and sometimes band with angels to save us from ourselves and dangerous liaisons. We've all had lifesaving miracles happen when emergencies arise. In these instances, our soul team creates supernatural occurrences that shift phenomena to rescue us. Our souls are the real super-heroes that try to steer us from bad actions, as they know we will eventually pay for

them, like me in my dark zone. So, listen to what is soulfully honorable and stay harmonious within every experience, whatever it may be.

Our inner voice is our consciousness hooked into self-knowledge. Meanwhile, it's humans with no spark and no conscience hanging out in the underworld who can't hear their own secret-self-dispatch, and still their soul is always trying to reach them but sometimes they're too far gone. While life is not easy these days, once we feel sparked it doesn't matter what's real or not easy. All that matters is that we shift our perception into a zone where nothing is impossible. To believe 100% in an outside chance, we are invested true magic that begins to work for us.

Years ago, I had a conversation with an artist at a cocktail party for Artists Against Abuse, although self-abuse would be a better description in his case. This artist told me that he felt dead in his soul and couldn't paint or do anything but drink; he was in agonizing emotional pain. I asked him what he'd do if he weren't this disabled and he said he wanted to build his own artist's studio with his own hands. He then went through all the reasons why this was impossible, mostly because of a lack of money. I let him go on while I absently started tapping the heart center of his chest, which appeared to be the source of his paralysis. He just let me do it while he ignored my tapping him for the entire conversation. I was opening up his tight closed heart chakra and told him that he had to build this studio, no matter what it took. Maybe it was a combination of the tapping and the words, but a spark

was transmitted, and he grasped it.

The next day this artist went to apply for a mortgage and from this one action the universe got involved. Miraculously, a dear friend heard that he was going for a mortgage without a dime to his name and showed up to co-sign the loan. My artist friend built his studio and his life woke up, his art started selling and he recently told me he longer drinks to excess. He instead eats well and is so roused that he wishes there was more time in the day. Interestingly, this man calls me every few years for some reason or other and on the day he told me how sparked he was, I was almost done writing this book. I was just as sparked as he and knew his call was a confirmation that the success we feel from doing what we really want to do is the way we make room for grace to come in and assist our ideas in finding wings.

Once in a while we hit bottom in order to transcend and yes, I hate it too. I hate the clouds of doom that sometimes pass overhead and try to color my world. I hate that I have to be strong and hold my own when anxiety has sneaked in the back door and is messing up my psyche. I hate that I constantly have to begin again after I spend hours cleaning up the mess a crisis has made. I hate that I have to control Bad Bitch, and I admit that I love her energy, her drive, her honesty, her edginess and her ability to call shit the way it is. I hate the way we get into trouble every time she lets loose and I admit it feels better when we rise above reactions. Then again, my Bad Bitch energy is part of my spark and we must take the best from all aspects of ourselves as we're a

team. I still need her to remind me of that side of myself, because her wildness is my fuel. Together, we're a duo that's in perfect balance as the Bad Bitch with a Good Witch soul.

Bad Bitch does not try to fit in and refuses to do what's not scintillating. Still, she couldn't care less what the world thinks about her, as it's not between her and them. She's used to not being understood and is used to how things sometimes get twisted around, as the lesson is not to take it personally. She invested in untangling her mistakes while forgiving herself for them and gets mad as Hell and refuses to stay down, rejecting rules that make no sense. She will pull out a bullhorn to express herself in the face of all wrongdoing and will always look to find another way even if it kills her, because her truth hooks into her credibility. She has powerfully made peace with herself for her degrading participation in all aspects that are between her and her Gods to absolve.

All along, it was about embracing the shadow instead of fighting it. The hymn Bad Bitch energetically hummed was: *Embrace* Me! I did. In discovering the magic our shadow side hides, we must see what it needs and who it wants us to become beyond our dusk. When I cuddled my darkness, I discovered and owned myself as I am. I came to adore all aspects of myself and used everything I've got going on as grist for my mill. In truth, we're all a full-on actuality of pure alchemy and a lightning bolt of magic, which means that all the ingredients in our mix are part of the Abracadabra conversation that we thrive on. It also means that there's a

force inside us that has a say-so on our quality of life no matter what and so we must beam our magic on that say-so with everything we've got.

Morphing in and out of realities, mindsets, and our holiness, we are growing into and out of ourselves over and over as we fall down rabbit holes like Alice. Here we talk to beings who may or may not exist in this reality and we run along in wonder chasing our imagination, as we're playing with prospects. In these times, we live in full-on uncertainty and solely on the enchantments we dream of. The message right now is to dream beyond all the monotonous realities, beyond the failures, beyond hardship, and into the places of promise. Dream and keep dreaming, no matter what. Dream of goodness for all concerned, dream of peace and freedom, dream of relief from pain and suffering, dream of love and happiness, and believe that the impressions of these dreams will inspire us to find our way.

And as far as struggling goes, struggle well, as when the butterfly is breaking out of her cocoon. She has to struggle, which forces fluid into her wings, so when she exits, she can fly. There are times during the struggle when the butterfly pauses. She's not giving up, but just collecting energy for the next push towards her breakout. The butterfly does not push until she's ready, she waits and dreams, and when she hears her calling then she pushes. That's where we are right now—we're smack in the next push. One day soon, that push will lead to the blink where we are free. So please don't get lost in the rules, the storylines, wondering if things are right or

wrong—just do what you love and what impassions you. It doesn't matter if you have a platform, a million followers or just one, or if you're a nasty bitch—it only matters what you take from this life and how you use it. It matters what you learn as you go, especially what you let go of and what you reach for more of. Mostly in the end, all that matters are the ways we embrace ourselves through all of it.

P.S. For all the things I've ever done that weren't good enough, kind enough, honest enough, or compassionate enough—that wasn't me.

ACKNOWLEDGMENTS

I am thankful . . .

Thankful for my great spirit that held me when I could not hold myself. Thankful to my Bad Bitch, the radical rebel who brought me to Hell where we excavated the Good Witch to save us. I am grateful for my survival skills, the ones I made up that have enchanting pathways. I am grateful for Malorie a.k.a Lori Barbaria and her childish aspects, her great heart, her wonderment and her embrace of my spirit into herself.

I am blessed . . .

Blessed by my husband, Joe, my soul mate, my love, and my best friend. My son, Max, a wizard, a visionary, a truth-sayer, an energy mover, a young man who knows love and inspires me every day. His life partner, Suzanne Diaz, a radical beauty I adore. My brother, Robert Schnur, who is surviving his grief. His wife, Soumaya, whose hand I always hold across the ethers. My sister-in-law, Darlene Barbaria, known as Arty D, whose selfless service has taken care of the elders—may she be blessed for this.

I [illegible]an sister Judy Lavine, whom I have never physically met, but who has assisted me through the grid lines to make magic happen. My astrologer, Stephanie Azaria, Heidi Banks my Spiritual Sister and healing consultant, and all the healers I've met along this way. My accountant, the secret saint Arish Dalal who told me not to worry about finances for a year and to do what I love because I deserve it. I listened to him.

I bow to the relatives and friends . . .

I bow in total grace and am beyond grateful to all my friends and teachers, all my relatives, cousins, and kindred spirits.

I'm grateful to Jason at Polgarus Studio for laying out this book. And to Scott Bluedorn for the beautiful cover drawing and Redbirds Designs for the cover layout.

I'm thankful to Lou Sagar, owner of The Alchemist Kitchen, my favorite shop in Manhattan, for including me in his family of Alchemists.

I am touched and loved spiritually . . .

Touched by my mother, who is constantly hanging around, sending me messages, and kvelling in happiness with